Europeans
in
Africa

STUDIES IN
WORLD CIVILIZATION

Consulting Editor:
Eugene Rice
Columbia University

Europeans in Africa

Robert O. Collins
University of California, Santa Barbara

Alfred A. Knopf   *New York*

THIS IS A BORZOI BOOK
PUBLISHED BY ALFRED A. KNOPF, INC.

First Edition

9 8 7 6 5 4 3 2 1

ISBN: 0–394–31004–7

Library of Congress Catalog Card Number: 78–124664

Manufactured in the United States

FOR CATHY, RANDY, AND ROBBIE

Preface

In 1930 Halford Lancaster Hoskins published his *European Imperialism in Africa* (Holt, Rinehart & Winston, New York, 1930) in a series entitled The Berkshire Studies in European History. The purpose of this brief study, indeed the purpose of the Berkshire series, was to provide a synthesis of the subject for college and university students of history. Professor Hoskins' book was widely used for several decades by students and teachers of history because of its concise, yet inclusive, treatment of Europeans in Africa, which had hitherto appeared only in more ponderous volumes dealing with Africa or in narrow monographic studies ill-suited for the introductory student or the classroom. Professor Hoskins, of course, presented European imperialism in Africa strictly from a European point of view, which helped to continue the European-oriented tradition of historical scholarship about Africa that dominated African studies until the 1950s. Much has occurred during the generation since Hoskins wrote. Not only has decolonization and independence come to Africa, but also major advances in both the history of Europeans in Africa and the history of Africa itself have made the earlier works obsolete and irrelevant for present students of Africa or, for that matter, of Europe.

Specifically, historians of Africa and Europe have, during the past decade, taken a fresh look at the European contact, partition, and administration of Africa as archival materials have become available in both continents. They have uncovered new information from which new interpretations have been fashioned. Of even greater importance has been the appearance of African history itself, which has dramatically altered the way in which historians have traditionally viewed Europeans in Africa and has placed the ethnocentric proclivities of earlier works by European and American historians in more proper perspective.

This short volume is concerned with Europeans in Africa. It is not a history of Africa. In this sense, the subject reflects the approach of European-oriented historians. This treatment of a traditional subject, however, is an attempt to include the products of modern historical scholarship, not only about European overseas expansion, but also about African history itself. Europeans have played a decisive role in the development of modern Africa, and the student should have available for his use a concise summary of their activities that incorporates the many new materials and interpretations.

I deeply appreciate the sound advice of Roger Williams, Lewis Gann, Robert Griffith, Martin Legassick, Eugene Rice, Roger Louis, and Ralph Herring, who have all taken precious time to read the manuscript. Their comments have immensely improved my original draft, for which we all can be grateful. My thanks also to John Wiley and Sons, Inc., for permission to use material from my introduction to *The Partition of Africa: Illusion or Necessity,* which appears in Chapter 3 of this volume.

R. O. C.
Santa Barbara, California

Spring 1970

Contents

Introduction

Most early writers of universal history adopted one of two tactics: they wrote the story of their own civilization and called it a history of the world, or they wrote theological history, the story of how God ruled his earthly kingdom. Medieval Western historians did both at once. They identified their own past with the history of the human race and gave it meaning and value by believing that this past was the expression of a providential plan.

Early efforts to write universal history failed because mankind had no common past. The pre-Columbian civilizations of America attained their splendor in total isolation from the rest of the world. Although the many different ancient peoples living around the Mediterranean were often in close touch with one another, they had little knowledge about civilizations elsewhere. The Chinese knew accurately no other high civilization. Until the nineteenth century, they regarded the ideals of their own culture as normative for the entire world. Medieval Europe, despite fruitful contact with the Islamic world, was a closed society.

The fifteenth-century European voyages of discovery began a new era in the relations between Europe and the rest of the world. Between 1600 and 1900, Europeans displaced the populations of three other continents, conquered India, partitioned Africa, and decisively influenced the historical development of China and Japan. The expansion of Europe over the world gave Western historians a unifying theme: the story of how the non-Western world became the economic hinterland, political satellite, and technological debtor of Europe. Despite an enormously increased knowledge of the religions, arts and literatures, social structures, and political institutions of non-Western peoples, Western historians wrote a universal history that remained radically provincial. Only their assumptions changed. Before 1500, these assumptions were theological; by the nineteenth century, they were indistinguishable from those of intelligent colonial governors.

The decline of European dominance, the rise to power of hitherto peripheral Western countries such as the United States and the Soviet Union and of non-Western ones such as China and Japan, and the emergence of a world economy and a state-system embracing the planet have all created further options and opened wider perspectives. Historians of the future will be able to write real world history because for good and ill the world has begun to live a single history; and while this makes it no easier than before to understand and write the history of the world's remoter past, contemporary realities and urgencies have widened our curiosity and enlarged our sympathies, made less provincial our notion of what is relevant in the world's past, and taught us to study non-Western civilizations with fewer ethnocentric preconceptions. One of the intellectual virtues of our time is the effort to combine a conviction of the relativism of our own past and present beliefs with an affirmation of the civilizing value of the study of non-Western cultures. Among teaching historians good evidence of this commitment has been the wish to include non-Western materials in the traditional Western Civilization survey course and the growing interest in teaching World Civilization.

Professor Collins' book on Africa in the age of European imperialism is one in a series of twelve paperbacks to be published under the title *Studies in World Civilization*. A second study will be devoted to precolonial Africa. Of the ten other studies in the series, one book will deal with early and one with modern developments in China, Japan, India, the Middle East, and Latin America. The purpose of this series is to help teachers to broaden their survey courses in whatever directions they think desirable and to introduce students early in their careers to the historical experience of non-Western peoples.

Professor Collins' perceptive essay is a splendid example of one way to do this. It is a study in cultural diffusion, of how Europe, principally in the nineteenth and twentieth centuries, exported ideas and techniques to Africa and of how Europeans and Africans attempted to fit them to African conditions and African needs. It therefore tells us much about both African and European history. To European history it contributes a dramatic chapter on imperialism. In an African perspective, it is the story of peoples conquered, colonized, and enslaved, of the destruction of traditional social and cultural forms and the creation of new ones, and of a colonial interlude—one of enormous consequence—between the African past and the African present. But perhaps we best read Professor Collins' book as a study in the violent cultural collision between European and non-European cultures, the shock of which was extremely painful and can still be felt. Of several relevant lessons, one is especially useful to students of Western Civilization: by studying the conflict between nineteenth-century Europeans and black Africans we both sharpen our awareness of some distinctive aspects of the Western past and widen our understanding of our roles in present conflicts.

EUGENE RICE
Columbia University

Europeans
in
Africa

Chapter 1

The
Portuguese
in Africa

Africa first came under the European sphere of influence in antiquity when the Mediterranean coast of northern Africa was incorporated into the Hellenistic and Roman empires. During those centuries North Africa was exposed to European culture, government, and religion, and the northern littoral of Africa became more closely associated with Europe than with the vast sub-Saharan regions to the south. In the seventh century the European influence in North Africa was suddenly broken when Muslim armies swept out of Arabia on their holy mission to spread Islam. Advancing along the coast, the Arabs conquered all of North Africa and laid siege to Europe itself. Isolated from Africa and the Middle East by the Arabs, Europe turned in upon itself, more concerned with recapturing the order and the security that had vanished with the Roman empire than with expending its energies and resources in foreign lands. As power and prosperity returned to Europe, however, the interests of Europeans in Africa revived. With power came the desire to spread the teachings of Christ among the heathens. With prosperity came the demand for, and the resources to acquire, African and Oriental products. In the past the Europeans had been forced to deal with the Arabs, who not only held North Africa, but also controlled the trade routes to the Orient. Impervious to Christianity, the Arabs were not prepared to give up control of trade with the East to European merchants. Hoping to circumvent Arab middlemen, Europeans, particularly the Portuguese, began their tentative explorations along the African coast in search of an alternate route to the East. Led by a new and vigorous dynasty, the House of Aviz, the Portuguese were ready to carry the Christian crusade against Islam to Africa and to convert the Africans to Christ for the spiritual and material profit of the Portuguese nation.

The Portuguese crusade was not an immediate success. In 1415 a Portuguese expeditionary force captured Ceuta, across from Gibraltar, but the Portuguese were unable to penetrate farther into the Muslim states of North Africa. Nevertheless, the governor of Ceuta, Prince Henry, the third son of King João I of Portugal learned of the Sudanic states across the Sahara, speculated on their wealth, and pondered on their relations with the pagan Africans farther south who bartered gold and slaves for the salt and Mediterranean products of the Muslim merchants. Unable to defeat the Muslims of Morocco, Prince Henry sought to outflank them, and from 1415 until 1460 he organized the systematic exploration of the Atlantic coast of Africa.

There has always been a demand in Europe for Asian and African products—spices, sugar, silk, gold, and ivory. As the feudal and city states of medieval Europe experienced economic growth, the demand for Oriental products sharply increased among an expanding leisure class. The supply seldom met this demand, inflating the price and stimulating merchants to deal in Asian and African goods at high risk but higher profits. The leading Christian merchants came from the maritime city-states of northern Italy, particularly from Genoa and Venice. By the end of the fourteenth century the Venetians had come to dominate the Eastern trade at the expense of their Genoese rivals. Throughout the fifteenth century Genoese navigators, sailors, and merchants therefore searched for new opportunities to gain control of the trade. They were experienced, highly skilled, and aware of the earlier expeditions which had hesitantly probed the inhospitable coast of Morocco and had landed in the Canary Islands. As a result, Prince Henry employed them to conduct his expeditions down the coast of Africa.

IN WEST AFRICA The Genoese and Portuguese captains prepared the expeditions to sail south under the watchful eye of Prince Henry. Each expedition was to be a step in a deliberate and systematic plan of exploration that would provide information and test nautical equipment for future expeditions. Henry hoped first to make contact with the peoples of West Africa, to convert them to Christianity, to enlist them against the Muslims, and to trade for their gold. The profits from the gold would help finance Portuguese expeditions to the Indian Ocean and the Orient. Here the Portuguese hoped to find the legendary Christian kingdom of Prester John and, in alliance with him, divert the wealth of the East from the Muslim merchants of the Levant and North Africa to Portugal and Europe.

This was a grand design with all the cartographic sweep to fire the imagination of Portuguese captains and make more endurable the sacrifice and hardships of dangerous seas and alien lands. It was the beginning of that Portuguese maritime tradition which inspired the great epic poem of Camões, the *Lusiad,* and the current speeches and pamphlets, if not the practice of Portuguese colonialism. In 1419 the island of Madeira was discovered, but then the pace of exploration slackened. Although the Azores were sighted between 1427 and 1431, Portuguese captains failed to double Cape Bojador, the limit of European navigation, until 1434. A spate of new discoveries followed. Cape Blanco was rounded in 1441; and the mouth of the Senegal River and Cape Verde were reached in 1445. The coast was no longer inhospitable desert, but luxuriant forest, inhabited by blacks who were not Muslims. It was called Guinea. Interest in the abundant vegetation, gold, and slaves stimulated further exploration. By 1460 Portuguese ships had reached Sherbro Sound in Sierra Leone.

Henry's death in 1460 momentarily checked the Portuguese advance along the West African coast. In 1469, however, a Lisbon merchant, Fernão Gomes, was given a monopoly on trade along the Guinea coast beyond Cape Verde on condition that he explore 100 leagues, or about 400 miles, of new coastline each year. By 1475 his ships had reached the island of Fernando Po and had pressed on across the equator. In 1483 one of Portugal's greatest navigators, Diogo Cão, arrived off the mouth of the Congo River. Cão named the river Zaïre, erected a stone pillar to commemorate his discovery, and landed emissaries to proceed to the court of the king of the Kongo. Later, returning up the coast, Cão seized four Kongolese hostages, who were taken to Portugal for an introduction to Portuguese civilization. In 1488 Bartolomeu Dias doubled the Cape of Good Hope, and a decade later Vasco da Gama followed him around the Cape and sailed up the East African coast and on to India. Nearly a century after Prince Henry had launched Portuguese overseas enterprise, Islam had been outflanked, and the way to the riches of the East had been opened. The Portuguese had succeeded in establishing contact from Cape Verde to Mombasa. What relationships would now evolve from the interaction of Europeans and Africans?

ON THE GUINEA COAST The discovery of the sea route to the East did not immediately eclipse Portuguese enterprise along the Guinea coast. Merchants and soldiers in considerable numbers followed the navigators to trade and to rule, but they either died, were assimilated into the local populations, or returned, hopefully enriched, to the sunshine of Lisbon. Thus, Portuguese energies were confined to trade, exclusive trade that envisaged no commercial competition, either European or African. As early as the 1480s João II claimed sole rights over 2,000 miles of the Guinea coast, concentrating Portugal's commercial interests in Upper and Lower Guinea.

Upper Guinea stretched from Cape Blanco to Sierra Leone, where the Portuguese focused their commercial efforts at Arguin, just south of Cape Blanco. Initially Arguin was an entrepôt for the gold mines of the interior, but the gold trade never developed. The merchants began to deal in slaves instead, but even the slave trade declined after half a century. Arguin then lapsed into disuse as a commerical center. Thereafter, Portuguese trade shifted to Santiago Island, from which Portuguese merchants crossed to the coast. Some traded and returned to Portugal; others settled at such outposts as Cacheu and Bissau. Many became renegades who preyed on the merchants. A few were missionaries sent out from Santiago to convert the Africans and to die.

Despite the freebooters, trade seems to have flourished. The African chieftains welcomed the opportunity to exchange gold, slaves, and ivory for European cloth, glass, and hardware. Moreover, there were no powerful, centralized African states in Upper Guinea, and the small chieftaincies of the interior shrank from a trial of strength with the Europeans as long as the commercial transactions were advantageous and the Portuguese made no attempt to transform economic ties into political control. Similar feelings motivated the Portuguese. As long as trade was profitable, the Portuguese Crown had no desire to expend its limited resources on territorial conquest and therefore urged Portuguese officials in Upper Guinea to maintain peaceful relations.

In Lower Guinea, which stretched from Sierra Leone to the Cameroons, Portuguese policy followed a different course. Portuguese merchants could not move throughout the hinterlands with freedom and security. The density of the forest hindered communications; malaria, feared on the coast, was usually fatal in the interior; and the African polities were stronger and less willing to permit aliens to wander around without any control. The most powerful state on the Lower Guinea coast was the Kingdom of Benin, whose ruler, the Oba, exerted control from Lagos to the Niger Delta. In 1486 the Oba had welcomed Portuguese traders, who established a factory* at Gwato; he exchanged ambassadors and listened to Portuguese missionaries, but he did so as a superior who both permitted and controlled Portuguese activities. Throughout the rest of Lower Guinea Portuguese traders were forced to confine their commercial transactions to fortified stations, like the famous castle São Jorge da Mina, known today as Elmina. Communication between the factories by sea or armed escort along the shore, and attempts by traders to penetrate into the interior were strongly resisted by the Africans, who had good reason: they had to protect the Ashanti gold mines. Because of the mines, they had more to lose than their less restrictive neighbors in Upper Guinea. Eager for profits, the Portuguese were forced to rely on African traders to deliver gold from the mines. It was undoubtedly these same agents, often powerful political figures, who confined the Portuguese to tenuous footholds on the coast. Nevertheless, Portuguese trade at São Jorge da Mina was the richest of the Guinea coast; the value of the gold trade alone was estimated to be $300,000 annually.

IN THE KONGO   Just as Santiago Island off Cape Verde became the center of Portuguese trade in Upper Guinea, the equatorial island of São Tomé off Cape Lopez became the focus of Portuguese activities between the Guinea coast and Angola and particularly with the Kingdom of the Kongo. Colonized by a motley collection of renegades, officials, criminals, merchants, and slaves, São Tomé became an important slave and sugar market, whose inhabitants sometimes cooperated with, but usually undermined, Portuguese policy in the Kongo to their own advantage.

Portugal possessed no territorial aspirations in the Kongo. King João II regarded Diogo Cão's seizure of four African hostages in 1484 as an opportunity to make an alliance with their king, the Mani Kongo,

---

* A European factory in Africa was not a manufacturing plant where products are made, but a place where a commercial agent, known as a factor, lived.

convert him and his people to Christianity, and then to use Portugal's favored position to reach Christian Ethiopia. Presumably impressed with the wealth and power of Portugal, the Kongolese hostages returned in 1485 with Diogo Cão to the Kongo, where they undoubtedly helped to clear the way for the Mani Kongo's favorable response to Portuguese overtures. The Mani Kongo called for Portuguese missionaries and technicians to instruct his people. In 1490 King João dispatched three ships carrying priests and artisans who were to evangelize and to instruct, but not to conquer. The mission was an instant success. The Mani Kongo, his son Affonso, and many courtiers were baptized, and Portuguese craftsmen began to impart their skills to the Kongolese. Unfortunately, these auspicious beginnings were not followed by consistent contact or regular assistance. The resources of Portugal were not unlimited, and the discoveries of Vasco da Gama turned Portuguese energies eastward, leaving behind in the Kongo a vacuum that was soon filled by adventurers from São Tomé, whose trade in slaves produced a powerful faction that sought to undermine both Kongolese and Portuguese authority.

In 1506 Mbembe Nzinga, or Affonso I, succeeded his father as king of the Kongo. Unlike his people, he was a devout Christian and a sincere admirer of Portuguese culture. He enthusiastically attempted to adapt the best aspects of Portuguese civilization to his culture, without obliterating Kongolese traditions or arbitrarily replacing indigenous institutions with those of the Portuguese. His heroic efforts, however, were frustrated from the beginning by the intrigues of the Portuguese in São Tomé and internal dissension within the kingdom. At the time of Affonso's accession to the throne, economic life in the Kongo had already become dominated by the slave trade, which was largely in the hands of the freebooters from São Tomé. Despite the king's efforts to restrict slaving, the trade rapidly increased until virtually all the Portuguese, including the missionaries, were engaged in buying and selling slaves. Receiving neither moral support from the missionaries nor political assistance from

Portugal, the authority of the Mani Kongo was gradually eroded away by the São Tomé slavers who played upon the eternal disputes over succession to the principal offices of the state.

King Manuel of Portugal finally responded to Affonso's pleas for assistance in 1512. He sent an expedition consisting of five ships under the command of Simão da Silva, whose *regimento,* or set of instructions from the king, affirmed for the first time the Portuguese intention to Europeanize an African polity. Simão da Silva was to help Affonso further Christianity and to introduce Portuguese law, military organization, and court ritual. He was to reform those Portuguese living in the Kongo by curtailing the slave trade and expelling undesirable traders and renegades. He was to encourage legitimate trade and stimulate geographic exploration. From an ally and a partner, the Kingdom of the Kongo was to be transformed into a Portuguese protectorate.

Although the grand design of the *regimento* provided a theoretical foundation for future Portuguese colonial policy, it had little immediate impact. Simão da Silva died shortly after reaching the Kongo, and even if he had lived, the implementation of the *regimento* was far beyond the resources or the interest of Portugal. Affonso did not appear willing to accept the *regimento.* Despite his belief in the benefits of European civilization, he did not intend to convert the Kongo into an African imitation of Portugal. He rejected the legal code as too harsh. He never initiated the military reforms. He did not encourage the teaching of Portuguese skills except to the secretaries at the national and provincial levels. He adopted, however, the exterior ritual of Portuguese court life, without reorganizing the political structure of the kingdom to conform to that of Portugal. In the end Affonso's relations with Portugal appeared more eclectic than doctrinaire.

The failure to implement the *regimento* marked a turning point in Portugal's relations with the Kongo. Thereafter, Lisbon appeared content to permit the São Tomé faction to control affairs in the kingdom. The

São Tomé slave traders totally dominated economic and social life in the Kongo, and the other Portuguese inhabitants of the island obstructed communication between the Kongo and Lisbon, virtually isolating the kingdom. As the king's authority disappeared from the provinces, war and the slave trade depopulated the interior. Affonso died early in the 1540s, and with him vanished the vision of Afro-Portuguese cooperation.

Revolts, civil wars, and succession struggles followed his death. Periodic, but futile, attempts were made to restore order. The first Jesuit mission appeared in 1548 but failed to bring stability or moral ascendancy. In 1570 Portuguese troops arrived at the request of Mani Kongo Alvaro to defeat the Jagas, a migrating tribe from the interior. The Jagas had suddenly appeared in the Kongo in 1568, defeated the Kongolese forces, and occupied the capital, São Salvador. In gratitude for driving the Jagas from his kingdom, Mani Kongo Alvaro acknowledged the suzerainty of Portugal, but Portuguese interests had already shifted away from the Kongo southward to Angola. By the end of the sixteenth century the unity of the kingdom had dissolved, and most vestiges of Portuguese life had disappeared; by 1700 the capital was deserted and its churches empty. The road to ruin in the Kongo had been paved by the good intentions of the Portuguese. Lamentably, Affonso's faith in the power of Portuguese civilization had proved unfounded. In the end Portuguese resources were simply insufficient to meet the requests of the Mani Kongo in Africa while building a far-flung empire in the Orient. Without sustained assistance from the Portuguese Crown, the kings of the Kongo could not prevent the slave trade from destroying their kingdom.

IN ANGOLA Although Portuguese slave traders had long operated south of the Kongo, Portuguese attention was not directed to Angola until the decline of the kingdom and the founding of Luanda in 1576 by Paulo Dias de Novais, a grandson of Bartolomeu Dias. Here Portuguese policy contrasted sharply with her system of pacific penetration and alliances practiced further north. From the beginning the Portuguese sought territory as well as trade, resulting in campaigns of conquest and direct, authoritarian rule. To be sure, there was no single, powerful king in Angola comparable to the Mani Kongo through whom the Portuguese could exert their influence for profit or control. The African sobas, or chiefs, were numerous and petty, yet similar political institutions in Upper Guinea had not led to the widespread acquisition of territory. Indeed, this change in the relations between the Portuguese and the Africans was not so much the result of conscious policy as of the character of the occupation by Paulo Dias and the need of military intervention to protect the slave trade. Moreover, these campaigns did in fact produce a continuing resistance which stimulated state formation when hitherto autonomous chiefs subordinated themselves to a superior political authority thereby acknowledging a wider political allegiance.

In 1560 a Jesuit mission visited the court of the Ngola, the king of the Kimbundu people, who inhabited the land between the Dande River in the north and the Cuanza River in the south. The expedition was a failure, but Paulo Dias de Novais accompanied the Jesuits. Upon his return to Lisbon he secured, with Jesuit support, a *donatário*, or proprietary lordship, from the court. Dias was to settle colonists in Angola, maintain a garrison of four hundred men, and construct three fortresses. In return he was to receive hereditary rights to all the land he could conquer; the Jesuits were to acquire a populous region for proselytization; and Portuguese influence was to be consolidated in Angola at no cost to the royal treasury.

Dias returned to Angola with his followers in 1575. He founded Luanda, constructed forts along the Cuanza River, and then embarked on a bloody campaign against the forces of the Ngola in search of souls and silver. He found little of either, but his campaign and indiscriminate use of force set the character of future Portuguese activities in Angola. Paulo Dias died in 1589, leaving behind disorder and hostility from which only the slave traders prospered. Three years later the Crown took up the legacy of Dias. Francisco de Almeida was appointed governor general, and a colonial administration was established to carry out the occupation and economic exploitation of Angola. His objectives were much the same as those of Dias. Gone were the days when the Portuguese court regarded Africa as a land in which to trade on a basis of mutual interest and respect for African institutions.

By the beginning of the seventeenth century the future course of Angola had been largely determined. By 1604 acting governor Manuel Cerveira Pereira had demonstrated that Angola contained no productive silver mines. Thereafter, for the next three and a half centuries, Portuguese traders, officials, and missionaries concentrated on the slave trade. Although Portuguese administration did not extend far inland, half-caste Portuguese and African traders, *pombeiros*, pressed deep into the interior to barter with African chieftaincies. Slaves were procured in a variety of ways: sometimes Portuguese governors demanded them as taxes, but most often they were refugees or captives from local wars that were provoked by traders. These wars were carried out largely by Africans in alliance with the Portuguese. With their sparse numbers the Portuguese, even with firearms, could not have conquered Angola without African allies who in turn sought to use the Portuguese against local rivals or for immediate gains. The results were large numbers of captives and refugees who vanished into slavery. Everyone participated in the slave trade: the settlers, the officials, and even the missionaries.

The Portuguese colonists in Angola were never numerous, but they soon comprised an exclusive caste virtually independent of the royal administration that supposedly governed the colony. In fact, officials had few incentives to exert their authority; poorly paid, they often supplemented their meager salaries with the profits from the slave trade in the pursuit of which they frequently ignored directives from Lisbon and acted almost as independently as did the colonists.

The Jesuits dominated missionary activities throughout the colony but particularly in Luanda, the modern capital of Angola. They not only educated Africans and mulattoes for minor posts in the bureaucracy, but they also regarded themselves as the protectors of the indigenous population. Unhappily, the Jesuits thought the most effective way to protect the African was to sell him into slavery, from which he would learn the dignity of labor and be introduced to Christianity. Supported by such reasoning, the Jesuits vigorously participated in the slave trade, frequently competing with officials and colonists who became their bitter rivals. For over three hundred years the slave trade conditioned life in Angola, accounting for 80 percent of the colony's commerce before 1832 and determining attitudes and assumptions that linger in Angola to this day. Despite a host of pious pronouncements, Portuguese policy in Angola amounted in practice to the indifferent exploitation of Africans and the paternalistic acceptance of those mulattoes or few Africans who adopted Portuguese values.

In 1641 the Dutch captured Luanda as part of a wider European conflict, only to surrender seven years later to a force from the Portuguese colony of Brazil under the command of Salvador Correia de Sá e Benavides. After the defeat of the Dutch, Salvador de Sá set about to reconstitute Portuguese authority in Angola. When he returned to Brazil in 1652, he had not only revived the supply of slaves to South America, but he had reasserted Portuguese control in Angola, although the Portuguese never regained their former commercial monopoly in Africa. Thereafter, Portuguese rule in Angola was chiefly characterized by constant bickering among the Jesuits, officials, and colonists. Toward the end of the seventeenth century successful Portuguese forays into the interior increased the slave trade. These continued fitfully for another hundred years, slowly extending Portuguese authority and depopulating the land. Otherwise, little changed in Angola in the eighteenth and nineteenth centuries. The proceeds of the slave trade were displayed in the pretentiousness of the mansions of the settlers and official buildings, and in the saintliness of ecclesiastical edifices. But beyond these isolated gardens of luxury spread a ravaged land upon which lived an exploited people.

This pattern of life in Angola extended from the beginning of the colonial occupation until the twentieth century, with only brief intervening periods of realism and charity on the part of a few remarkable men. The seventeenth century had Salvador de Sá—tough, disciplined, and forbidding. The eighteenth century had Francisco de Sousa Coutinho, who arrived in Angola in 1765, and concluded that the future prosperity of the colony could not be based on its depopulation. In place of the slave trade he envisaged the colonization of Angola by the hardy yeomen of Portugal who, by developing the colony, would end the exportation of its African population. Like Affonso I, Coutinho was either too naïve or too prescient a man to serve successfully as governor-general of Angola in the eighteenth century. The economy of Portugal depended on the Brazilian plantations, and those plantations needed Angolan slaves. Sousa Coutinho's reforms, like those Simão da Silva was delegated to implement in the Kongo, were undermined by Portuguese castoffs of Angolan society. By the end of the century Coutinho's attempts to bring humaneness out of depravity and order out of corruption were conveniently forgotten; his failure was symbolized by the continuous and profitable trade in slaves.

The decline of Portuguese civilization in Angola was further exemplified by the decreasing number of missionaries combating the sins of their secular countrymen. By 1800 there were only ten fathers and twenty-five parish priests, half of whom were African. Like converts everywhere, the African clergy were more zealous than the Portuguese, who often lapsed into penitential sloth or communicant luxury. Most of the Jesuit or Capuchin missionaries preferred to remain in Luanda rather than hazard health and life in the interior. But in the harsh world of the colony, the missionaries did perform an educational service and, occasionally, a spiritual one. In fact they

represented the only spark of intellectual enlightenment in an otherwise dark and soulless European
tyranny, but in the end the missionary offered little
more to the Africans than "a disembodied doctrine,
many of whose disciplines were distinctly distaste-
ful." *

IN EASTERN
AND CENTRAL
AFRICA

Although Portuguese beginnings in eastern Africa
followed at first the pattern established in the west,
economic interests, geographic factors, and African
resistance ultimately resulted in Portuguese rule
adopting quite a different character. In March 1498
Vasco da Gama anchored in Mozambique harbor and
then proceeded north along the coast, calling at Mombasa and Malindi before setting sail for India. To the
astonishment of the Portuguese, they found in the
Zanj city-states of the coast a Swahili civilization that
was materially comparable to sixteenth-century Portugal. Its city-states—Pate, Malindi, Mombasa, Kilwa,
Zanzibar, Pemba, and Sofala—had stone houses,
quays, markets, and an atmosphere of prosperity, if
not elegance. Only in the development of military and
naval technology were they inferior to the Portuguese.
The importance of this military weakness was magni-
fied, however, by political division. Each city-state
was ruled by a prince who jealously guarded his political and commercial independence against his rivals. In
their dealings with the Zanj city-states, the Portuguese tried to establish the same pattern of relationships that they had employed along the Guinea coast.
They founded forts and factories for the purpose of
trade, preferably in alliance with the local authorities,
but if necessary they used force of arms. The use of
force unfortunately shaped future relationships between the Portuguese and the East Africans and ultimately undermined their commercial interests.

In 1505 Francisco de Almeida sailed for the East to
establish a Portuguese commercial monopoly in the
Indian Ocean. Those city-states that did not submit

---

* James Duffy, *Portugal in Africa* (Cambridge, Mass.: Harvard
University Press, 1962), p. 66.

peacefully were sacked, and Portuguese authority was imposed on the inhabitants. But since Portuguese interests were concentrated farther east in the Orient and India, the Swahili and Arab traders were able to continue their commercial activities, interrupted only by infrequent Portuguese attempts to assert their political rule or a mercantile monopoly. As elsewhere the Portuguese in East Africa acquired control of the coast by capitalizing on the fierce rivalries among the city-states and by using their superior military technology. Their numbers were, however, small: at the most there were never more than a few hundred Portuguese in the coastal towns and they were unable to maintain control because of internal revolts and intrusions by the Dutch and English into Portugal's Eastern empire. By the mid-seventeenth century the Arabs from the state of Oman who had resisted Portuguese influence in Arabia were able to carry their struggle against the Portuguese from the Persian Gulf to East Africa, and by the end of the century the remnants of Portuguese power collapsed. In 1698 an expedition from Oman captured Fort Jesus, the great fortress at Mombasa and the symbol of Portuguese rule, and thereafter Portuguese authority was restricted to the coast south of Cape Delgado in the colony of Mozambique.

On the coast of southeast Africa the Portuguese concentrated at Sofala, the gateway to the gold mines of the Rhodesian plateau, and Mozambique Island, the most important port of call between Lisbon and India. Sofala owed its existence and development to the gold trade, which never matched Portuguese expectations in volume, but the gold trickled out in sufficient quantity to keep hopes of great fortunes alive. A few Portuguese grew rich; most did not. The others were content to trade and garrison the coastal stations. Except for a few isolated journeys into the interior, the Portuguese made no effort to impose their authority in the hinterland or to claim the gold mines. Even in 1531, when a trading station was established at Sena on the Zambezi with the promise of a second at Tete farther upriver, the Portuguese sought only to increase the export of gold by getting nearer to the supply. As in Guinea they came up the Zambezi to trade, not to conquer. They hoped the Africans would be their allies, not their subjects, and they respected the political integrity of the African authorities in the hope of peaceful relations with them.

THE PRAZEROS The retirement and disinterest of the Crown in Zambezia did not mean the end of Portuguese activity. Missionaries, adventurers, and *prazeros* were involved in the interior, although some priests were more concerned with ministering to the Portuguese than proselytizing among the Africans. In 1560, however, Gonçalo da Silveira arrived in Mozambique specifically for the purpose of converting the heathens. He journeyed to the court of the Mwanamutapa, where he baptized the king, his wife, and three hundred courtiers. He was then assassinated at the instigation of Muslim traders. His martyrdom was later not only avenged by the Barreto expedition, but other missionaries came to take his place. The Dominicans were next in the field, working throughout Zambezia proselytizing, converting, and entrenching themselves at the court of the Mwanamutapa. The Jesuits soon followed, confining their activities to the coast. The missionaries failed in Zambezia, however. African intransigence, disease, and corruption undermined attempts at proselytization, while the political fragmentation, which had overcome the empire of the Mwanamutapa before the arrival of the Portuguese, made widespread conversion to Christianity by the people quite unlikely. By the end of the eighteenth and the beginning of the nineteenth century, the missionary effort in Mozambique had, for all practical purposes, collapsed, and the missionaries had disappeared.

In 1568 King Sebastião, ambitious and stubborn, became discontented with the meager profits of the gold trade in eastern Africa. He wished to control the mines as the first step to creating a vast Portuguese empire in the heart of southern Africa, to ruling the Africans, and to eliminating the Arabs as commercial and religious rivals. In 1569 the army of a thousand volunteers sailed from Brazil under Francisco Barreto to begin the conquest of the hinterland and to avenge the murder of Gonçalo da Silveira. After inordinate delays the army assembled at Sena in 1571, where malaria decimated the troops and Barreto himself. By 1573 only two hundred men were left. A year later a reorganized expedition of some four hundred men under the command of Vasco Fernandes Homen fought its way to the gold mines of Manica, only to discover that machinery and a disciplined labor force would be necessary to increase production. Further attempts to establish Portuguese control in the interior were discouraged by Homen's negative reports, and in the end the Portuguese acquired neither gold mines nor territory, but only the hostility of the Africans. Royal interest in the hinterlands was momentarily revived at the beginning of the seventeenth century, but limited resources and African animosity turned the dreams of imperial expansion in the hinterland into nightmares of frustration and failure.

As imperial expansion was forgotten and the Church dwindled into failure, official Portuguese expansion was eclipsed by unofficial activity in the form of the *prazo* system. Beginning in the late sixteenth century individual Portuguese soldiers and traders carved out great estates throughout Zambezia. Surrounded by their slaves and armed retainers, they lived in baronial splendor beyond the control of official Portuguese authority. In return for helping the Mwanamutapa and other African leaders in their endless tribal conflicts, these *prazeros,* as they were known, received grants of land and authority over the African population. They took African wives, created personal armies to extend and defend their domains, and virtually enslaved the African population. They were absolute masters who assumed the powers of African chiefs and lived in opulence in great houses built from the profits of their plantations. Although the Portuguese government outlawed the *prazero* system in 1832, the royal decrees were ignored until the end of the century, when these Zambezian warlords were finally broken by force and the *regime does prazos* was modified to suit the developing economy of Mozambique.

Before the *prazeros* came to their timely end, however, they had begun to engage more actively in the slave trade. Although the trade in slaves had long existed on the East African coast, carried on mostly by Arab and Swahili merchants, it was always small compared to that in Angola and the Kongo. In Mozambique the procurement of slaves was as erratic as the trade in gold, although slavery flourished on the plantations of the *prazeros*. But until the nineteenth century the demand for slaves outside East Africa was never as great as the need for laborers to farm the *prazo*. At that time Angola could no longer adequately supply the requirements of the New World, and a big boom in the Mozambique slave trade developed despite a decree in 1836 that abolished the trade. Only by British diplomatic and naval intervention was the trade restricted, and even then it continued in French plantations on the Mascarene Islands under such euphemistic names as "contract labor"; Napoleon III prohibited such devious schemes in 1864.

By the seventeenth century Portugal was no longer the only European power in contact with Africa. Holland, France, and England successfully challenged the Portuguese and in turn replaced them as the principal European participants in trade and politics along the coast of that continent. Nevertheless, the trans-Atlantic slave trade inaugurated in the Portuguese period remained long after Portugal's authority was reduced to a few isolated posts and, in fact, set the pattern of relations between the Africans and those Europeans who assumed the mantle of the Portuguese monopoly. When the Portuguese had first appeared on the coasts of West and East Africa, Portuguese civilization was not much more advanced than were many African cultures. The great scientific discoveries and the technical and industrial revolutions in Europe, which created an enormous disparity of power between European and African states in the nineteenth century, were still far in the future. True, the stubby caravels of Vasco da Gama were clearly superior fighting ships to the lateen-rigged dhows of the Indian Ocean, and the muskets of the Portuguese were an advance over African spear and shield. Nevertheless, Portuguese political, religious, and social institutions made little or no contribution to African civilizations. The *regimento* of King Manuel I was not much of an improvement over the political and social structure of the Kingdom of the Kongo. Christianity, as presented by Portuguese missionaries, failed everywhere to attract the Africans who found greater comfort in their traditional religions or in Islam. Even the social customs of the Portuguese had little relevance to a relationship which had degenerated into a trade in slaves. Moreover, the Portuguese were not colonizers. Portugal had no surplus population so that only those Portuguese seeking converts or riches were attracted to the hostile environment of Africa. Gold yielded profits but not Christians. The slave trade produced both and soon came to dominate Portuguese relations with Africans, undermining the traditional political and social institutions, on the one hand, while obstructing attempts to introduce the more enlightened and humane aspects of Portuguese civilization on the other. Where African authorities requested material and spiritual assistance, Portugal possessed neither the resources to support her best intentions nor the power to control her more unscrupulous subjects. Where African authorities were forced to submit, Portugal had neither sufficient numbers of able officials to replace indigenous rule with efficient alien administration nor the strength to sustain orderly government. The result was political stagnation and social disorientation that produced the tragic, but profitable, legacy of human degradation that Portugal bequeathed to her European successors.

Chapter 2

Africa Before the Scramble

Portugal could not sustain her imperial initiative. Her resources were limited, her numbers few, and her religious leaders uncompromising. Despite the profits of trade and the exploitation of slave labor, Portugal simply did not have the economic strength to monopolize Eastern commerce or the men to staff her far-flung outposts. From the small population of Portugal, relatively few men went to Africa, and fewer returned. Those who did not die from disease took wives from among the local women. They soon produced a mulatto class that came to represent the Portuguese empire overseas; these settlers were neither as efficient nor as committed to Portuguese civilization as their fathers were. Throughout the sixteenth century they manned Portuguese vessels, though they had inadequate nautical education and insufficient experience, which resulted in a decline in Portuguese seamanship. By the seventeenth century Portuguese ships in African and Eastern waters were no match for their Dutch and English rivals.

Once the Portuguese could no longer dominate the sea lanes, they could no longer control the land. They had come to Africa and the Orient to trade, not to colonize, but their policy of forging strong alliances with powerful indigenous rulers was undermined in

Africa by the slave trade and in India by religious intolerance. The famous phrase attributed to Vasco da Gama, "I seek Christians and spices," was not mere rhetoric. If the slave trade destroyed any hope of a strong Portuguese ally in the Mani Kongo, the religious intolerance of the Portuguese alienated the Muslims, the Hindus, and even the Nestorian Christians of India. By the end of the sixteenth century the Portuguese imperium was greatly overextended and tottered from internal weakness on the verge of collapse. It did not take Portugal's European rivals long to discover the frailty of her empire.

In 1577 Sir Francis Drake became the first English captain to circumnavigate the globe. Drake rounded Cape Horn and pillaged Spanish ports along the Pacific coast. After refitting in northern California, he crossed the Pacific and Indian oceans and discovered that the trade routes of the Portuguese were defended only by scattered forts usually beseiged by hostile African and Asian enemies from the interior. Drake's revealing voyage was soon followed by ominous events in Europe. In 1580 Philip II succeeded in uniting the Crowns of Portugal and Spain, enlarging at a stroke his imperial holdings, but exposing Portugal to the detestation and fear with which the Protestant powers regarded Catholic Spain. Previously, Portugal's preoccupation with overseas expansion had kept her relatively free from European entanglements, but now she was regarded as a potential enemy at home and her colonies a legitimate prize abroad.

Among the first to profit from Portugal's newly exposed position was the House of Orange. The power of the Dutch House of Orange was based on trade. While they were still subjects of the Spanish Hapsburgs, the Dutch merchants had acted as the Northern distributors of the goods the Portuguese brought back from the Orient. When the Dutch, led by the House of Orange, revolted against the Hapsburgs late in the sixteenth century, this source of trade with Lisbon was cut off. In order for the House of Orange to retain its power and the Netherlands her independence from

Spain, Dutch merchants had to sail to the East themselves and take over Portuguese commerce there. The revelation of Portuguese weakness overseas showed that it would be possible to follow the routes of the Portuguese merchants without having to force a new passage through the unknown wilderness of northwest America. Moreover, the first tentative Dutch and English expeditions to the Orient were making details available on sea routes to the East, the hazards of navigation in Eastern waters, and the Eastern ports.

THE DUTCH   The first Dutch fleet sailed for the Orient under Cor-
IN AFRICA   nelis de Houtman at the end of the sixteenth century. His reconnaissance was followed by a series of Dutch voyages undertaken by merchant syndicates and companies for the purpose of trade in the East Indies and for the negotiation of commercial treaties with local rulers. Not only did the Dutch have better ships than the Portuguese, but they were superior sailors and more astute merchants. From both policy and practice the Portuguese could not tolerate Dutch interlopers; open conflict was not long in coming. In 1601 the Dutch decisively defeated a Portuguese fleet in the harbor at Bantam in West Java province. The following year the Dutch East India Company was founded. The Dutch Crown granted the Company a commercial monopoly from the Cape of Good Hope east to the Strait of Magellan, and it transformed individual Dutch enterprise in the East into a great national effort to combat the Portuguese, to create a mercantile monopoly, and to present a united front to the indigenous rulers.

At first the Dutch concentrated their naval power against Portuguese trade and factories in the Indian Ocean. Within a decade the Portuguese fleet in the East had been destroyed, and in 1611 the first governor-general arrived at Bantam to organize the administration of the Dutch East Indies. Preoccupied by empire building in the Orient, the Dutch left Spanish and Portuguese interests in America and West Africa alone until the Dutch West Indies Company was founded in 1621; thereafter, the struggle against the Iberian powers was carried to the South Atlantic. The Company first confined its activities to the Spanish Main and Portuguese colony of Brazil, which was largely in Dutch hands by 1637. At that time the prosperity of Brazil had become dependent upon the importation of African slave labor, and the Dutch, who were anxious to profit from their conquest, set about to ensure a regular supply of slaves from West Africa to the Western hemisphere. Although they had established after 1600 a few small trading posts on the Guinea coast, the Dutch factories were of little consequence in comparison to Portuguese holdings in Guinea, the Kongo, and Angola. Rather than attempt to meet the demand for slaves from these inadequate factories, the Dutch simply captured those of the Portuguese. By 1642 Portuguese forts in Upper and Lower Guinea, São Tomé, Luanda, and Benguela were in Dutch hands. Although the Portuguese were never able to reassert their control along the Guinea coast, they were able to reconquer first Brazil and then, with the Brazilian expedition of Correia de Sá e Benavides, Angola and São Tomé. Thereafter, the Dutch West Indies Company concentrated on supplying slaves from West Africa to the plantations in Latin America and the Caribbean as part of a triangular trade among Europe, Africa, and the West Indies. This extremely profitable trade attracted the attention of the English, however, and soon the Dutch found their newly won position under attack.

At first the Dutch tolerated English competition in the East and West Indies. They did not wish to alienate a formidable ally in the struggle with Spain. Moreover, English traders were neither as numerous nor the English East India Company as powerful as their Dutch counterparts. By 1650, however, the Spanish threat had receded, and the number of English and other European merchants had multiplied. Under the influence of seventeenth-century economic theory, European rulers had come to regard all commercial rivals, Protestant as well as Catholic, as a threat to the nation-state.

MERCANTILISM
AND
COMPETITION

Commonly known as mercantilism, the economic doctrine of the time, conceived in an age when capital was scarce, measured the wealth of a country in terms of a favorable balance of trade. It concluded that a state should pursue policies of international trade designed to obtain a favorable balance as reflected in the accumulation of hard money or bullion. Exports were encouraged since they brought gold and silver into the country, and imports were discouraged since money left the country to pay for them. Politically, mercantilism provided justification for strong political control by centralized government that could regulate the flow of commerce. Economically, it precipitated commercial conflict as each European state sought to gain a larger share of gold and silver. In England and France officials became increasingly alarmed to observe their national stocks of bullion pass out of their countries to the Netherlands in order to pay for tropical products from the Indies. To prevent the gold drain and to increase the influx of precious metals, both the English and French governments encouraged their own merchants to deal more in overseas trade by acquiring tropical products for the European markets in direct competition with the Dutch. Not only did the kings of England and France grant royal charters and monopolies to national trading companies, but they frequently invested their personal fortunes in commercial enterprises. Regulations were increasingly enacted or decreed to limit trade between the colonies and the mother countries to their citizens in ships flying the national colors.

Mercantilism had a profound effect on European activities in West Africa. The prosperous plantations of the Americas were dependent upon a regular and increasing supply of African slave labor to meet the steady growth in the number of plantations. In the past the Dutch had been willing to provide the slaves. After 1650 the doctrine of mercantilism, as well as the considerable profits derived from the slave trade, thrust the English and French into competition with the Dutch for a share of the slave trade.

The economic principles and profits that stimulated

English and French traders also motivated merchants from other European states. Traders from Sweden, Denmark, and Brandenburg operated on a much smaller scale than the major European states on the coast of West Africa, but their appearance did intensify the already fierce commercial and political competition. Under such highly competitive conditions, which made the slave trade a risky business, the European merchants employed chartered trading companies. These companies received a national monopoly from their respective kings that enabled them to compete as a group where they would have foundered as individuals. In 1660 the Company of Royal Adventurers into Africa received a royal charter from Charles II and was succeeded in 1672 by the Royal African Company. The French countered with the French West Indies Company founded in 1664.

The French concentrated their activities in Upper Guinea, where they had established posts as early as the 1630s, and at the mouth of the Senegal River, where they founded St. Louis in 1659. One by one the Dutch posts capitulated to the French; Arguin and Gorée fell in 1677, the latter becoming an important French naval base. Other French trading stations were established farther south on the Gambia River in the area known today as Portuguese Guinea and by 1713 the French had succeeded in replacing the Dutch in Upper Guinea. Unfortunately, however, trade in Upper Guinea never proved sufficient to sustain French efforts. The population of the Upper Guinea coast was too small to meet the demand for slaves; and even the ancillary trade in gum, ivory, and hides did not provide a sufficiently profitable substitute.

Southward from Gorée to the forests of the Gold Coast in Lower Guinea, the competition for slaves was less intense. Although these were well populated regions, in the north from the Gambia to Sherbro Island in Sierra Leone, the trade was in the hands of individual half-caste Portuguese traders who had long lived and traded from the safety of the labyrinth of coastal inlets and offshore islands. Protected by hundreds of hidden anchorages, they easily avoided all attempts, first by the Portuguese authorities and later by the European trading companies, to control their activities. Unable to intimidate these independent traders, the English and French merchant companies turned their efforts elsewhere. The Grain Coast and the Ivory Coast of Lower Guinea were not conducive to slave trade, since the shores were swept by storms and strong currents and there were no natural harbors and few landing places. In addition, the African population, though larger, was not well acquainted with the organization of trade or the methods of slaving. Although slaves could be purchased there, the numbers were insufficient to justify a European factory, particularly since more profitable opportunities lay to the east.

By the eighteenth century the slave trade of the Guinea coast was concentrated along the Gold and the Slave Coasts. Not only was the Gold Coast the headquarters of both the Dutch West Indies Company and the English Royal African Company, but it was also the scene of their greatest struggle for control. In 1664 the English had captured Cape Coast Castle from the Dutch, and in the first half of the eighteenth century their portion of the slave trade had steadily increased from one-third in 1700 to more than one-half by 1785. The Dutch merchants failed to respond to the competition. The victims of a general decline in the commercial position of the Netherlands throughout the world, the Dutch failed to remodel the management and organization of the Dutch West Indies Company to meet the changed conditions of African trade. Increasingly throughout the eighteenth century individual Dutch interlopers intruded into the monopoly of the company, trading in slaves, but contributing nothing to the maintenance of the forts and factories that protected the Dutch position on the Gold Coast.

Like the Dutch West Indies Company, the monopoly of the English Royal African Company was also invaded by individual traders mostly from ports in the west of England, but in 1750 the English merchants reorganized their African trade. The closed syndicate that had made up the Royal African Company was dissolved, and an association, the Company of Merchants Trading to West Africa, was created in its place to include all individual English traders who wished to engage in West African commerce. By admitting all those merchants who had hitherto been interlopers into a loose association, the Company of Merchants could enlist their financial support and political influence to maintain the strength of the English forts.

European companies on the Slave Coast developed differently than did the well-organized trading companies on the Gold Coast. The Portuguese had never been active along this stretch of the Guinea coast, and although known as the Slave Coast by the end of the seventeenth century, it was not a major supplier of slaves until the eighteenth and nineteenth centuries. Here the supply of slaves met the demand, and consequently commercial rivalries were less violent than they had been to the west. Forts were unnecessary, and without them, individual traders or small companies did not have to amalgamate into associations to defend their interests by constructing expensive installations. The individual trader only required a hulk to keep the slaves in for shipment and the good will of the African rulers on the mainland. These rulers not only collected duties from the traders, but also prohibited the construction of forts in order to limit European interference in African affairs.

Having destroyed Dutch dominance in the South Atlantic by 1713, Britain and France launched into a hundred years of war which ended in a British victory in 1815. Africa was only a subsidiary theater of operations in the war, but by the beginning of the nineteenth century the French holdings were confined to a few inhospitable outposts. In 1785 British slavers carried over 38,000 slaves to the Americas, or more than half the total of all slaves traded. The French were far behind, supplying only 20,000. The Dutch and the Danes hardly counted at all, carrying only 4,000 and 2,000 slaves respectively. The Portuguese role was insignificant. The Anglo-French wars of the eighteenth century, therefore, resulted in an astonishing increase in Britain's mercantile marine and the corresponding eclipse of her rivals. Moreover, the profits from the triangular trade they had seized from the Dutch and the wealth of the plantation economy that slavery made possible may have helped to finance the English Industrial Revolution of the late eighteenth century. Much of this ill-gotten wealth, however, appears to have been squandered on political patronage and personal consumption and thus was not employed as risk capital to finance British manufacturing industries. By 1800, Europeans in West Africa were preoccupied with trade in slaves, and this trade had now become completely dominated by British merchants.

THE SLAVE TRADE
The slave trade conditioned relations between Europeans and Africans on the coast of West Africa for nearly four hundred years. Throughout those long centuries the manner of trade evolved to meet the changing conditions produced by the interaction between Europeans and Africans. The first slaves taken from Africa by Europeans were snatched by small raiding parties from ships anchored offshore. This clumsy piracy was neither efficient nor effective, and European traders were not long in fashioning alliances with African chieftains for their mutual benefit. The Europeans offered goods that the Africans desired—firearms, liquor, hardware—in return for slaves. The negotiation of alliances evolved into a customary pattern of commercial exchange with traditional, even ritualistic, rules.

By the seventeenth century the system of trade by which the European merchant offered manufactured products in return for slaves was firmly entrenched along the coast; African rulers proffered slaves for those European goods that could strengthen their authority against commercial and political rivals. The slave trade thus imposed a new and pervasive factor in the rise and fall of African polities: it provided the opportunities for petty chieftains to become strong rulers, and for strong rulers to become powerful kings. Sometimes power came to the chiefs from the wealth collected for customs duties or from the profits of the trade itself. Other times the acquisition of firearms provided the means for African rulers to extend their domains by military conquest. Political survival on the coast came to depend increasingly on a chief's ability to protect his monopoly against attempted intrusion by European agents. To defend this monopoly a host of elaborate rules and customs developed which protected the integrity of buyer and seller.

The Africans were no less organized than the Europeans, and the chiefs and agents haggled long and hard in tough bargaining sessions, which were frequently interrupted with entertainment characterized by the giving of gifts, drinking, and ribaldry. Later the Africans began to tax the Europeans for the privilege of trading and to charge for services, such as ferrying goods and slaves from ship to shore and back again. The successful trader, whether African or European, learned not only the idiosyncracies of his counterpart, but the state of the trade along the coast and the complicated system of payments that prevailed. Slaving was a complex and speculative business in which the intricacies soon eclipsed any humanitarian considerations. Hardened by the passage of time and faceless captives, the traders soon came to regard the slaves as just another commodity from which to render profit. Their callousness toward human life was proportional to the volume of their business, so that the passage of time marked a decline, not an improvement, in human relations.

During the many years of the trade probably no less than nine million and not more than twelve million African slaves landed in the New World. A greater number of slaves left Africa than arrived in the New World, however, since many slaves perished during trans-Atlantic passage. In the end probably thirteen million (although some historians estimate twenty to forty million) slaves were taken out of

Africa.* Countless others were lost in the raids and wars for captives. Although slave trading began as a trickle in the fifteenth century, the trade increased to nearly a million in the sixteenth century, to three times that in the seventeenth, until its peak in the eighteenth century during which at least six million slaves reached America. Throughout the early decades of the nineteenth century the numbers steadily declined until the effects of the abolitionist movement finally brought the trade to a halt in the 1880s. By that time, however, nearly two million more slaves had reached the New World.

The impact of the slave trade upon Africa remains unclear and controversial. In the Kongo, Angola, and Mozambique, the long and disastrous record of the Portuguese is well known; the testimony of the Portuguese themselves clearly demonstrates how the trade eroded the fabric of African society, corrupted political institutions, and undermined the authority of the traditional rulers. The effects in West Africa are less clear, however. The coastal chiefs jealously guarded their monopoly against European attempts to penetrate the interior and to intervene in their customary markets. Europeans had long traded in the principal towns of the coastal states of Dahomey and Benin, but after three hundred years on the shores of Lower Guinea, they had never even visited Kumasi, the capital of the powerful Ashanti Confederacy, or Oyo, the capital of the Yoruba Kingdom of Old Oyo. Thus, the evidence from the European sources on the internal dynamics of the forest states of the Guinea coast is extremely limited, and the African sources have yet to be adequately collated and analyzed.

In their struggle against the slave trade, the nineteenth-century abolitionists and humanitarians assumed that the rise of the West African forest states was attributable to the wealth derived from the trade,

---

* For the most recent discussion on the statistics of the slave trade, see Philip D. Curtin, *The Atlantic Slave Trade: A Census* (Madison, Wis.: University of Wisconsin Press, 1969), esp. pp. 265–275.

just as their fall was the result of a moral decay generated by the sale of fellow Africans to European slavers. Since the slave owners justified slavery on economic grounds, the abolitionists sought to combat their position by an economic argument that has been uncritically accepted in our own times: The states of Benin, Oyo, Dahomey, and Ashanti acquired the strength to expand and to impose their authority upon their neighbors through the economic prosperity derived from the trade. Similarly, these states lost their strength through the destruction of the slave trade by European forces and the sapping of the state's moral fiber by the internal use and sacrifice of slaves.

Recently, historians of Africa have begun to take a fresh look at the slave trade in Africa and to challenge the traditional interpretation. Although individuals prospered and African magnates increased their power, African societies that engaged in the trade probably did not profit. The slave trade caused a diversion of labor from the production of food and clothing to unproductive slaving, and since these subsistence economies had little accumulated wealth upon which to draw, the margin of subsistence narrowed. Thus, the slave trade lowered the standard of living in general and increased the precariousness of life. In addition, political factors seem to have been as important in the rise and fall of West African states as were economic conditions. The decline of Benin appears to have resulted not so much from cultural and moral degradation as from the failure of Benin to adapt to the dynamic, external forces represented by the slave trade that allowed her outlying provinces to gain wealth and assert their autonomy, if not their independence. Similarly, the dissolution of the Kingdom of Old Oyo in the nineteenth century seems to have been as much the failure to resolve internal political problems as the result of slave raids. Undoubtedly, as more information is acquired on the constitutions and political organization of the forest states, the previously advanced economic rationale will recede into better perspective.

The influence of seventeenth-century mercantilism

on the slave trade died hard. Statesmen, planters, and even the general populace understood the great wealth that the West Indian plantations contributed to the British economy. That this wealth was bought at the price of human suffering was for the most part conveniently overlooked. Moreover, they never really experienced the degradation of servitude or witnessed the horrors of the Middle Passage between Africa and America. There were nearly ten thousand slaves in England, but they were mostly domestic slaves who had accompanied their masters to Britain as personal servants. As part of a household in which they performed services of trust and skill, these slaves were usually treated humanely, if not with affection, which was a striking contrast to the treatment of slaves in the West Indian plantations who, as field hands, suffered all the indignities of beasts of burden. Consequently, the arguments of the proponents of slavery were more easily accepted by Englishmen who never saw its practice on remote islands. The principal justification for slavery was the immutable right of property; slaves were like horses, to be bought or sold and to be exploited. Those who assumed the inferiority of the African also assumed his eternal damnation, so that it made little difference what happened to him. Many Catholics accepted the position of the Jesuits in Angola that the conversion of the African was best accomplished by laboring on behalf of Christian plantation owners.

In the eighteenth century virtually every European writer or philosopher in sympathy with the ideals of the Enlightenment protested at one time or another and in a variety of ways against slavery and the slave trade. At the same time, the concept of the "noble savage" helped to offset the image of the African as barbaric and to readmit the Negro into the brotherhood of man. The observations of European explorers at the end of the century demonstrated that Africans were not simply wild savages. In 1765 an organized campaign was launched against slavery and the slave trade by a small group of Englishmen led by Granville Sharp, Thomas Clarkson, and William Wilberforce. From small beginnings the abolitionist movement assumed massive proportions, particularly after the Declaration of Independence by the American colonies in 1776 removed the support of North American slave owners from the powerful West Indian lobby in Parliament. Coincidentally, the West Indies began to play a smaller role in the English economy, as England started to experience the effects of industrialization. But despite economic considerations, the abolitionist movement was fundamentally humanitarian, and its greatest weapon was virtue; against this moral force slavery and the slave trade could not prevail. In 1772 slavery was declared illegal in England by Lord Chief Justice Mansfield; in 1807 Parliament forbade British subjects to engage in the trade; and in 1833 slavery was abolished throughout the British Empire. Other nations soon followed Britain's example: the United States, Sweden, and the Netherlands prohibited the slave trade in 1808, 1813, and 1814, respectively.

EUROPEAN
EXPLORATION

More than any other factor, the slave trade drew Europe to Africa. The slave trade was not, however, the sole reason for European interest in that continent. The eighteenth century was an inquisitive and cosmopolitan age. This spirit of inquiry extended to the lands beyond Europe, stimulated by descriptions of exotic lands and strange peoples from travel books which found their way into the literature and scholarship of the century. The passions generated by the campaign against the slave trade provided powerful themes for poetry and drama. Freed slaves who lived in England, such as Ignatius Sancho and Olaudah Equiano, wrote of the miseries of the trade and life in Africa, generating both sympathy for abolition and also widespread interest in Africa. Even the increasing demand for tropical products was not solely the result of the profit motive. Some, like the tomato, were introduced for their decorative appearance. Other exotic plants were eagerly sought to enhance the grounds of stately homes in that great age of gardening. The work of the great Swedish botanist, Carolus Linnaeus, for example, encouraged his students, Andrew Sparrman and Carl Thunberg, to travel extensively in South Africa to collect plants and to observe the land and people. And in the Royal Botanical Gardens at Kew, England, established in 1760, the tropical plants of Africa were the most highly prized.

The attention of eighteenth-century Englishmen was first focused on the unknown tropics in the Pacific. In three successive voyages conducted between 1768 and 1778, Captain James Cook explored the great expanse of the Pacific, its archipelagos, and the fringes of its continents. He not only opened the Pacific to man for geographical study but he stimulated other exploration, in part because his voyages confirmed the tradition of government support for exploration. At the same time, the Scottish explorer James Bruce set off for the interior of Ethiopia in search of the source of the Nile. In February 1770 Bruce reached Gondar, capital of Ethiopia, and spent two years observing the Ethiopians and their land and visiting the springs of Gish, the source of the Blue Nile. He returned through the Sudan and Europe to England in 1774. The account of his exploration, *Travels to Discover the Source of the Nile,* appeared in 1790. Few believed all that Bruce had to say, but even fewer ignored him, and his work inspired later explorers.

Joseph Banks, who had accompanied Cook on his first voyage, was a wealthy man of high social position who became a powerful influence on exploration, particularly in Africa. Rich, sensible, and energetic, he was elected President of the Royal Society at the age of thirty-five and held that position for the next forty-two years. In 1788, in collaboration with twelve politically powerful and wealthy friends, Banks established an Association for Promoting Discovery of the Inland Parts of Africa, commonly known as the African Association. The founders were motivated principally by curiosity about the unknown, but they also passionately believed in "the utility of enlarging the fund of human knowledge." Toward that end they sponsored African exploration.

The African Association commissioned Simon Lucas, the Oriental interpreter at the Court of St. James, to make his way into the interior south of Tripoli, and John Ledyard, an American who had sailed on Captain Cook's last voyage, to explore from Cairo to Sennar on the Blue Nile and then westward to the Niger River. Within a year Ledyard died in Cairo. Although Lucas never passed beyond the coast, he acquired a wealth of information on the Fezzan in southwest Libya and on the lands to the south. His explorations further resulted in the Association's interest in the Niger River, about which Europe knew little. Reports of great Sudanic commercial cities on the river had long circulated in Europe, investing such cities as Timbuktu with a romance they ill deserved in the nineteenth century and making them the goal of explorers. Moreover, no one knew where the Niger rose, and geographers had been alternately identifying it with the Senegal, the Nile, and even the Congo rivers.

The African Association was determined to resolve the Niger riddle. From 1791 to 1792, on behalf of the Association, Major Daniel Houghton penetrated to Bambuk. He was followed in 1795 by the Scottish physician, Mungo Park, who reached the Niger at Segu. Park was the first Englishman to penetrate deep into West Africa. His book, *Travels in the Interior of Africa,* which first appeared in 1799, is a narrative of intrepid adventure that made him a hero, although his contribution to discovery and geography did not warrant such esteem. Nevertheless, few men did more than Park to popularize the quest to learn about the African interior or to combat the image of a dark continent populated by savages. After Park, European explorers pressed into Africa with increasing frequency. William George Browne reached Darfur province in 1792 and returned to El Fasher in 1794. Frederick Hornemann reached the Fezzan in Libya in 1798. James Guy Jackson explored Morocco in hopes of capturing the trans-Sahara trade. Henry Salt followed in Bruce's footsteps into the hinterland of Ethiopia in 1805 and returned on a second mission in 1810, which won him wide acclaim in London society and held out prospects of trade and intercourse between Africa and a Christian power. Finally, between 1813 and 1815 Johann Ludwig Burckhardt, a Swiss, traveled in Nubia and up the Nile River to Shendi, then eastward to the Red Sea, and across to Mecca and Medina; his perceptive observations of the northern Sudan are set down in *Travels in Nubia*.

African exploration was also popular outside of England. In Germany the scholarly journal *Allgemeine Geographische Ephemeriden* meticulously reported information on African peoples and geography. The Germans, however, did not have economic interests in Africa, so exploration was not utilitarian for them. Until the latter half of the nineteenth century, therefore, German explorers entered Africa for the most part under British auspices.

The French, on the other hand, were very active during the late seventeenth and eighteenth centuries. By the end of the seventeenth century French explorers and traders had penetrated four hundred miles up the Senegal River to Galam and in the first quarter of the eighteenth century inland from Bissau to the Futa Jallon. Trade in tropical products was never profitable, however, and even trade in slaves was never sufficient to meet the demands of the French West Indies. Defeat followed commercial decline. At the end of the Seven Years War with Britain, France lost all her possessions in West Africa except Gorée and Albreda; she recovered St. Louis in 1779 but had neither the strength nor the interest to return to the interior. The Napoleonic Wars nearly eliminated French outposts on the coast. France was unable to control the sea lanes, which prevented her from defending her colonies. Gorée fell to the English in 1800 and St. Louis in 1817, but French interest in Africa was not dead. In 1798 Napoleon Bonaparte invaded Egypt, routed the Mamluk defenders at the Battle of the Pyramids, and occupied Cairo. Even before Bonaparte turned to the East in search of victories, influential Frenchmen had considered Egypt a potential field for French enterprise. In 1769 Duc Etienne François de Choiseul, for example, expressed his belief that Egypt would be proper compensation for French losses in the West Indies. Later, in 1797, Talleyrand argued the advantage of having colonies in the Asian and African continents and specifically recommended to Bonaparte that the occupation of Egypt would result in French control of the overland trade with India. As in West Africa, however, the failure of France to control the seas doomed the French occupation in Egypt. Unable to obtain reinforcements and supplies from Europe, Bonaparte abandoned his troops and returned to Europe, leaving behind a French garrison that ruled Egypt until its capitulation in 1801.

To France, Bonaparte's Egyptian adventure was without territorial consequence. To Africa, the French eruption was profoundly significant. Not only did Bonaparte provide a framework for colonial rule by establishing an administration of occupation, but he had come there intending to modernize the country by the application of European science and technology. In this sense he was more the precursor of the mid-twentieth-century colonial rulers than the imperialists of the late nineteenth century. Moreover, 167 scholars accompanied Bonaparte to Egypt and founded the famous Egyptian Institute. They began the study of Egyptian antiquities and compiled the famous *Description de l'Egypte,* which covered every aspect of the country and its people and proved a stimulus for further investigation in Africa and the Nile Valley. Egypt was never the same after the French intrusion. Neither was the French attitude toward Africa. The concept of *la mission civilisatrice,* which had its origins in monarchial France when the sword and shield of the Church were regarded as a civilizing influence, had a profound effect on the feeling of nineteenth-century Frenchmen toward Africa.

Napoleon's imperialism in Egypt, on the one hand, and the capture of French posts in West Africa by British forces, on the other, renewed English interest in consolidating Britain's commercial position along the coasts by securing geographical knowledge of the interior. Thus, in 1805 Mungo Park, accompanied by sailors, soldiers, and artisans, set out a second time for the Niger intending to follow it to its mouth. Park and only ten companions gained the Niger at Bamako. With four men he began the long journey downriver only to drown in the rapids near Bussa. His disappearance not only ensured Park a prominent place in Britain's pantheon of heroes, but it continued to excite the imagination of Europe about the mysteries of the African interior.

War between Britain and France resumed in 1803, and the long, tiresome struggle against Napoleon diverted the resources of the British government from African exploration. After Napoleon's defeat in 1815, however, the government once again supported expeditions. In 1816 the government sent Captain James Kingston Tuckey up the Congo River to determine its relation to the Niger. Tuckey's expedition did not go far; after encouraging the Congolese to trade with Englishmen, he retired to England without discovering the navigable Congo beyond the rapids and without throwing any light on the Niger question. Thereafter, attempts to reach the Niger once again shifted to North Africa. In 1818 Joseph Ritchie and George Lyon reached the Fezzan. Ritchie died, but Lyon returned to confuse the issue by claiming that the Nile and the Niger were, in fact, one river. Four years later a government-sponsored expedition by Dr. Walter Oudney, Major Dixon Denham, and Lieutenant Hugh Clapperton, R.N., set out from Tripoli and crossed the Sahara to Bornu, where the party divided. Denham marched to the southeast, exploring Lake Chad and the Shari River. Oudney died, but Clapperton pressed on southwestward toward the Niger. He failed to reach the river but visited Kano and Sokoto. Upon his return with Denham to England in 1825, Clapperton not only had information indicating that the Niger flowed into the Gulf of Guinea, but he had observed powerful Sudanic states in whose towns craftsmanship and commerce flourished. Excited by his reports, the British government immediately sent Clapperton back to Africa; this time, with his servant Richard Lander, he struck inland from Badagri on the Guinea coast. He reached the Niger at Bussa, crossed to Sokoto, but failed to convince the sultan of Sokoto to sign a treaty which would have prohibited the slave trade and encouraged legitimate commerce. Clapperton died in April 1826 on the return journey. Richard Lander managed to reach the coast and return to England, where he persuaded the Colonial Office to permit him and his brother, John Lander, to complete the work of Park and Clapperton. In 1830 they traveled down the Niger River from Bussa to the sea and proved at last that the Niger emptied into the Gulf of Guinea through the maze of delta channels known as the Oil Rivers.

Park, Clapperton, Denham, and the Lander brothers delineated for Europe the geographical outlines of the interior of West Africa. Others filled in the details. The Frenchman G. Mollien discovered the sources of the Senegal and Gambia rivers in 1818. His intrepid countryman René Caillié became the first European to visit Timbuktu and return. The Englishman Major A. G. Laing located the sources of the Niger River in 1822. Nevertheless, the very success of the Lander brothers diminished the interest of the British government in explorations from the coast of West Africa. The knowledge of the Niger's course lessened the zeal for discovery as a factor in Britain's commitment in West Africa; when this commitment was revived in mid-century, it came from the north across the Sahara. In 1850 the expedition of James Richardson and two Germans, Adolf Overweg and Heinrich Barth, left Tripoli for the Sudan. Richardson soon died; Adolf Overweg died in 1852; and then Barth wandered alone across the plains of the Sudan taking meticulous observations and collecting valuable information on Sudanic states from Lake Chad to Timbuktu. His travels and his accounts of them place him among the greatest of European explorers of Africa.

Second only to the slave trade, exploration was a prime motivation to impell Europeans into Africa. Although exploration was inextricably intertwined with the prospect of trade on the one hand and with exposing the horrors of the slave trade on the other, it also caught the imagination of those Europeans who were neither involved in commerce nor attracted by the crusading zeal of the abolitionists. The romance of African exploration continued to captivate the imagination of Europe during the second half of the nineteenth century when the slave trade was dead and the cause of abolition no longer required a European presence in Africa. By that time, however, the Christian mission movement took up where the abolitionists left off.

CHRISTIAN MISSIONS

The Protestant mission movement in Africa had its roots in the evangelical revival of the eighteenth century. For nearly half a century John Wesley had preached about the life of good works and the importance of religious experience. Wesley's impact was largely among the poor, the class least likely to take an interest in Africa, but which provided many of the nineteenth-century missionaries. Wesley's preaching also affected more influential groups, particularly those interested in evangelism within the established Church of England itself. Wealthy, socially prominent, and devout, the Anglican evangelists came to form a powerful pressure group in British society. Along with other Protestant evangelists they aroused the social conscience of Christians and helped to set a new value on human life. Irrespective of denominational differences, the evangelists worked assiduously for abolition and proselytization in Africa. In fact the two themes cannot be separated—abolition provided the stimulus for the introduction of Christianity in Africa and evangelism was the means to end the trade in human life.

Consequently, at the end of the eighteenth century a host of Protestant missionary societies were organized in England to carry the teachings of Jesus Christ to Africa as another weapon in the crusade against the slave trade. In 1792 the Baptist Missionary Society was founded, followed by the London Missionary Society in 1798, the Church Missionary Society of the Church of England in 1799, and the British and Foreign Bible Society in 1803. Thus, by the beginning of the nineteenth century numerous missionary societies joined the abolitionists, the traders, and the African Association in promoting the interest of Europe and, more particularly, of England, in Africa. Many of the members of these groups overlapped from one organization to another. The driving force was abolition, but from this core a host of peripheral efforts—ranging from exploration to trade and even to colonization—riveted Britain to Africa and laid the foundations for imperial initiatives.

CHRISTIANITY, COMMERCE, AND COLONIZATION

European colonization in Africa began as a product of abolition. The prohibition of slavery in 1772 had created a class of freed blacks in England just when the War of Independence in America required the resettlement of black loyalists who had fought for the British. Under the leadership of Granville Sharp and the antislavery movement, an attempt was made to settle freed blacks in Sierra Leone in a utopian colony optimistically called the Province of Freedom. The first settlers arrived in 1787, but disease, rain, and infertility of the soil decimated the black colonists. The Sierra Leone Company was thus created by Act of Parliament in 1791, and European administrators were sent out to govern the colonists in the hope, unfortunately vain, that orderly rule and technical advice would overcome the obstacles of nature. The Company and the colonists quarreled constantly. Not until the administration of Zachary Macaulay, governor from 1794 to 1799, was the colony firmly established.

The Company had hoped to profit from a legitimate trade with the interior, which never developed. In 1800 the Company received its first government subsidy in order to defray the expenses of administration. Thereafter, the British Treasury subsidized Company rule until 1808, when the British government took over Sierra Leone as a Crown colony for use as a naval base and dumping ground for slaves liberated by the anti-slave trade patrol of the Royal Navy. Thereafter, Sierra Leone grew under British administration as an outpost of European civilization in West Africa.

A settlement similar to Sierra Leone was established in Liberia by the American Colonization Society in 1821. Although ostensibly founded for humanitarian reasons, in fact, Liberia was the creation of a society and a government that were more interested in deporting an undesirable segment of the American population—the freed blacks in the southern states—than in performing an humanitarian act. As a result, although several communities were established, these were not given adequate support, and Liberia was left to develop with little diplomatic or financial assistance from America. Moreover, the United States, unlike the British government, never became directly involved in anti-slavery activities on the coast of West Africa.

The Act of Parliament of 1807 had prohibited British subjects from trading in slaves. To be effective, however, the legislation had to be enforced. In Britain this was no problem, particularly since the judicial decision of 1772 and the Act of Parliament affected few people. In Africa enforcement proved more difficult. The British Royal Navy was charged with the unenviable task of implementing the Act of 1807. A permanent naval squadron patrolled West African waters to halt the export of slaves in British vessels. The slaves freed by this squadron were taken to Sierra Leone where they became the core of that colony's population and, in later years, one of the most active missionary and merchant groups in West Africa. The patrol successfully limited the activities of British traders, but it did not restrict the trade in slaves. In fact, to meet the insatiable demand of the Americas, the number of slaves annually taken out of Africa increased sharply between 1810 and 1830, although the number of British slavers declined.

Unable to stop and search ships of other countries on the high seas, the British government sought permission to do so from France, Spain, and Portugal, whose subjects were most active in the trade. No nation has been more vigorous in her defense of the freedom of the seas, yet Britain in the early nineteenth century set out to limit this freedom by negotiating reciprocal search treaties with Spain and Portugal in 1817 and with France in 1831. Britain was able to overcome the objections of some nations through negotiations and international agreements; with others, like the United States, who refused to sign a reciprocal search treaty until 1862, she was not. Even the right to search did not curtail the trade, however, for the slavers devised a variety of means to avoid capture. In the end the Royal Navy anti-slave trade patrol proved a failure. Between 1825 and 1865 nearly thirteen hundred slave ships were captured and 130,000 slaves released, but nearly 2,000,000 slaves were transported to the Western Hemisphere in the same forty-year period.

Ironically, the failure of the preventive squadron to end the slave trade kept Britain committed to Africa at a time when the government's other interest in West Africa was waning. The discovery of the lower course of the Niger River had seemed to make further government support for African exploration unnecessary. Even the eighteenth-century economic arguments for government protection of trade appeared no longer acceptable or applicable. Individual traders had seemed to confirm the economic theories of Adam Smith by demonstrating the efficiency of their separate commercial activities in contrast to those of the monopoly companies, and their enthusiasm for free trade was reciprocated by the government, whose political agents on the coast produced little commercial advantage in return for their maintenance of the forts. It was much cheaper to withdraw the Crown agents and return the control of the forts to the merchants. By 1830 neither the African trade nor African exploration could have promoted continuing European involvement in Africa. The dearth of any strategic British commitment in West Africa and even the financial and human losses of the naval squadron from disease were employed as arguments for government withdrawal. Thus, at the time when the British interest in abolition, exploration, and legitimate commerce was diminishing, only the British government's long commitment to eradicating the slave trade kept Britain on the coast. The abolitionists were too strong to ignore and too earnest to deceive, yet the failure to end the trade by diplomacy or force had confronted the abolitionists with the need to search for a more positive policy to end this iniquitous commerce.

In 1822 Sir Thomas Fowell Buxton succeeded William Wilberforce as the leader of the anti-slave trade members of Parliament. In 1839 Buxton published an influential book entitled *The African Slave Trade and Its Remedy,* which recommended a positive policy to combat the slave trade. The policy is best characterized by the famous slogan Christianity, Commerce, and Colonization; and the Society for the Extinction of the Slave Trade and the Civilization of Africa was founded to carry it out. The Society hoped that by establishing European settlements in West Africa the colonists would, by example and experience, demonstrate the virtues of Christianity and the value of "legitimate" trade to the Africans. The slave trade would thereby be replaced, and African society reformed, by European technology and institutions. Although the idea of establishing English plantations in overseas territories was not new, Buxton and his followers regarded themselves as innovators by relying on such new devices as the steamship. Inspired by Buxton's policy and influence, the British government sent out a large expedition in 1841 to steam up the Niger, to establish a missionary station and plantation at Lokoja, and to open the interior to legitimate trade. The expedition was a disaster. Forty-eight of the 145 Europeans died within two months, and the mission was recalled. In one stroke disease destroyed Buxton's policy, but did not end Britain's commitment in West Africa. Instead, Buxton's failure resulted in the formulaton of new methods to terminate the trade, which ultimately led to the partition of West Africa.

Unable to eliminate the trade by Christianity, commerce, and civilization, the abolitionists and government alike fell back on the use of preventive action. The navy was employed more ruthlessly, as symbolized by Captain Denman's attack on and destruction of the slavers at Gallinas in 1841. More important, however, these decisions precipitated far-reaching changes in Afro-European relations. The recognition and acceptance of African authority, which had characterized dealings along the coast between Africans and Europeans in the eighteenth century, gave way to policies in which officials, traders, and missionaries intervened directly in African affairs. The subordination of African leaders into clients of English consuls, the extension of territorial jurisdiction by the English, and the increasing dependence of the administration on the profits of African commerce led inexorably to imperial control. The disaster of the Niger expedition in 1841 thus marked a watershed in English relations with West Africa. Henceforth, the British acquired obligations, the satisfaction of which were resolved by imperial rule.

TOWARD IMPERIAL CONTROL

The transformation of African chiefs from independent merchant princes into clients of British power was carried out through a network of treaties by which the chiefs agreed to abandon the trade in slaves. The treaties, as such, did not change the status of African chiefs, but the enforcement of them did. By the use of British power and influence, consuls such as John Beecroft, who was appointed to the Bights of Benin and Biafra in 1849, were not just ambassadors; they were representatives of the British government prepared to interfere with African rulers to stop the slave trade by diplomacy or, if necessary, by force. The British consuls and naval captains were supported after 1850 by British Christian and commercial interests. Already employed in theory, if not in practice, as instruments to fight the slave trade, they came increasingly under the protection of consular power. The defense of these interests alone frequently came to result in the extension of imperial influence.

By the early nineteenth century Christian missionary societies had been established to combat the slave trade by evangelization and education. Their influence strengthened in mid-century when those Africans who had been liberated from slave ships and deposited in Sierra Leone began to return to their homelands. They returned with the European skills and Christian religion that they had acquired during their sojourn in Sierra Leone. When they arrived at Badagri, Abeokuta, and Ibadan in Nigeria, the emigrants were treated honorably—their skills admired, their religion tolerated. The missionaries quickly followed the Africans and, like them, were hospitably welcomed for their technological knowledge, if not for their religion. In return for education and economic development, the missionaries insisted on an end to the slave trade and the opportunity to preach for Christ. They were content to train an African middle class, to whom the political power of the chiefs and the economic power of the European traders would eventually pass. They aimed to replace pagan cults and rituals with Christianity, and, provided Christianity was accepted, they were prepared to recognize that Africa should belong to the Africans. Unfortunately, this attitude did not last. In their desire to protect their missions and converts from the ravages of the wars in Yorubaland and the abuse of hostile chiefs in all areas, the missionaries increasingly turned for assistance to the counsuls along the coast who, in many cases, were anxious to expand British influence and control. At the end of the century a new generation of European missionaries came to Africa; as the religious counterparts of imperial officials and merchants, they curtailed African participation in the leadership of the Church.

From the beginning of the nineteenth century, the volume of legitimate commerce, particularly of peanuts and palm oil, steadily increased; between 1850 and 1874 it tripled in value. There was increasing demand in Europe for illumination and greater interest in personal cleanliness, which stimulated the manufacture of candles and soap, while the wheels of the industrial revolution required more and better lubricants. Led by enterprising merchants, British traders were active on the coast but were discouraged from pressing into the interior by the high mortality rate and the resistance of African middlemen. Then, in 1854, Dr. William B. Baikie's expedition up the Niger and Benue rivers proved quinine to be an effective prophylactic against fever. Once it had been demonstrated that Europeans could reach the interior of Africa and survive, the interest of the British government, missionaries, and merchants in the hinterland grew. The reports of Dr. Henrich Barth seemed to confirm the prospects of profitable trade in the interior of Africa, further stimulating this interest. The possibilities of direct access to the interior markets provided a powerful incentive for English encroachment on the coast, while African opposition to British traders pushing upriver simply stimulated efforts by British consuls to extend control over African societies in order to protect British commercial interests. A chain of expanding imperial protectorates began to grow from the older commercial enclaves, and the constant need for revenue to administer these possessions led to the acquisition of additional territory. Ministers were irresistibly caught up in a vicious circle. In order to finance an expanding colonial administration, they frequently acquired new territories for the purpose of deriving revenues from the proceeds of trade. British merchants were generally unhappy with this extension of empire. Previously, merchants dealt successfully with African middlemen, whose customary dues were preferable to paying imperial tariffs to support colonial treasuries in return for protection that the traders generally did not require. Only when the merchants journeyed into the interior did they need the protection of British battalions, but such ambitious projects were far beyond the resources of the small, independent coastal traders, who carried on the bulk of Britain's West African commerce. These efforts at interior trade gradually slipped under the control of large monopoly corporations.

Thus informal empire grew along the coast of West Africa due to a host of interacting factors, such as paying stipends to chiefs, employing the threat of force, and accepting the actions of consuls who pushed British influence forward in the context of frequently muddled policy. By 1870 the extension of imperial jurisdiction was no longer the result of prior agreement with African states, and the alliances and mutual agreements between Europeans and Africans were transformed for the most part into European influence and ultimate control. Informal empire created the footholds along the West African coast from which the British could compete with the French for control of the hinterland.

IE FRENCH IN WEST AFRICA

The defeats of the Napoleonic Wars had nearly extinguished French activities in West Africa, and although the interest of certain provincial merchant groups revived after 1815, France did not possess the pervasive commitment in Africa that held Great Britain to that continent. True, Africa remained one of the few areas still open to French expansion after the loss in the eighteenth century of her once extensive overseas empire, but she had neither active humanitarian interest in abolishing the slave trade nor private philanthropy to stimulate exploration and curiosity about Africa. Moreover, the government in France remained unstable. Alternating between republicanism and bourgeois monarchy, French colonial policy wavered between an egalitarianism that was hostile to colonial schemes and the vision of recapturing the imperial past. The imperial aspirations were only matched by their inconsistent and ill-considered application. Algiers was the first victim of this fickle policy.

With little thought and less excuse, the French invaded Algiers in 1830 for no reason other than to divert discontent from the misgovernment of Charles X by a spectacular and glorious military success in Algiers. Although the coastal cities of Algiers and Oran quickly capitulated, the invasion proved to be neither as glorious nor, in the long run, as successful as the French government had hoped. Having occupied the coastal plain, the French were forced to carry out a protracted and unpopular struggle in the mountains beyond against the hill people who were led by the redoubtable Abd-el-Kadir. Gradually the French established control in the hills under the skillful leadership of General Thomas Robert Bugeaud, who played upon the internal divisions within the Muslim tribes. In 1847 Abd-el-Kadir was captured, but dwindling resistance for another generation poisoned relations between the conquerors and the conquered. Nevertherless, with undeviating confidence, the French viewed the conquest of Algiers as the revival of ancient Rome's civilizing mission in much the same way that Mussolini regarded Italy's conquest of Ethiopia a hundred years later. The French developed the economy and communications, and by 1848 a hundred thousand Europeans were settled there, even though opposed bitterly by those Algerians who had lost their lands and rights.

Although the French remained in Algiers, the occupation did not save the monarchy. In 1830 Charles X was overthrown, and the revolutionary government of Louis Philippe, "citizen king" of the French, was much too absorbed by domestic difficulties and too discouraged by heavy French losses in Algiers to embark upon further African adventures. Nevertheless, French traders were not idle, spurred on largely by the rapid industrialization in France during Louis Philippe's reign. In 1843 fortified trading posts were established at Grand Bassam, Assinie, and Dabon on the Ivory Coast, while the former French fort at Whydah was reoccupied and commercial relations were reopened with the king of Dahomey. Although active, French traders remained few, and their stations were more outlets for French manufactured goods than outposts of the French empire.

The African policy of Napoleon III did not differ dramatically from that of his predecessors. Although nurtured by the past glories of his uncle and the need for success abroad to redeem the image both of France and of his own regime, the emperor did not follow a consistent pattern of overseas expansion, and in West Africa the initiatives were more the result of the activities of the men located there than of government policy. In fact, the French government had no central administrative agency, such as the British Colonial Office, to carry out imperial policies. The Direction des Colonies was a minor bureau attached to the Ministry of Marine; as a result, naval officers came to dominate the administration of French footholds in West Africa. Generally, these naval officers dismissed territorial expansion on the mainland as the product of commercial intrigue by petty traders. Only on the lower Senegal was a direct policy inaugurated, precipitated by the requests of French traders in gum and peanuts for protection against the powerful African states of the interior. Stimulated by the demand for soap, the exportation of peanuts from the Senegal had reached 5,000,000 kilograms by 1854, but since the Senegal Valley had proved unsuitable for European farmers, it remained a frontier for soldiers and traders rather than a colony for settlers like Algeria.

In 1844 the governor of St. Louis, Count Louis Bouët-Willaumez, urged French expansion up the Senegal River, but it was not until 1853, when Napoleon III sent out military reinforcements, that the French could move into the Futa Toro. The advance was led by Captain Louis Faidherbe, whose long governorship from 1854 to 1861 provided the continuity that had been absent until then from French administration in West Africa. Faidherbe not only created the Tirailleurs Senegalais, the elite African troops that formed the vanguard of the subsequent French march into the interior of Africa, but he sought to establish French authority in the vast, productive plateau between the Senegal and Niger rivers, which was controlled by the influential African Muslim leader Al-Hajj Umar. Al-Hajj Umar was a Tucolor notable who had made the pilgrimage to Mecca and had returned to establish a theocratic empire on the upper Niger and Senegal as a result of his political acumen, religious zeal, and military power. His political authority blocked the extension of French commerce upriver, and his religious influence threatened Christian control on the lower Senegal. Faidherbe set out to check Umar's advance and to extend the frontiers of French control into the interior. He was extraordinarily successful. The Futa Toro was occupied, and after the French established themselves at Dakar in 1857,

Faidherbe began to intervene in Cayor. By the end of his second governorship in 1865, he had established the pattern of French expansion in West Africa, and despite the delay created by the collapse of the Second Empire in 1870 and the insecurity of the early years of the Third Republic, his work represented the deepest penetration by European colonizers in tropical Africa and provided the basis for future French advances during the European partition of Africa.

EUROPEANS IN EAST AFRICA

Throughout the first three-quarters of the nineteenth century, Europeans had probed and consolidated their positions all along the western coast of Africa without actually laying claim to the interior. Except for a handful of explorers, few Europeans penetrated into the hinterland or acquired extensive territory as Faidherbe had done in the Senegal. This pattern of informal empire and influence on the coast, from which the tentacles of exploration groped toward the interior, was not confined to western Africa; in East Africa the prelude to partition closely resembled the pattern in the west. As in the west, the East African slave trade precipitated British intervention; Christian and commercial interests perpetuated it. As in the west, exploration stimulated public interest in East Africa; missionary and merchant followed the explorer into the hinterland. Finally the alliance between European and coastal African authorities gradually devolved into a clientage relationship. The reasons for the European partition of East Africa were very different than in the west, but the manner in which the foundations for the partition of East Africa were laid was very much the same.

Along the East African coast the Portuguese occupation of the sixteenth and seventeenth centuries disappeared before an Arabian power, the Imamate of Oman. Throughout the eighteenth century the Imams of Oman had exerted only nominal sovereignty over the Muslim, Swahili-speaking inhabitants of the coastal towns. During the first half of the nineteenth century, Imam Sayyid Said consolidated his rule in Oman and with British naval support defeated his principal rivals, the Jawasmi pirates of the Persian Gulf in 1810 and the Wahhabi tribes of Arabia in 1814. Then he reorganized the Imamate, introducing fiscal reforms and encouraging commerce, particularly the trade in slaves. Sustained by the demands of sugar plantations in the French Mascarene Islands east of Madagascar, the slave trade flourished, attracting the attention of the British abolitionists. At first the British sought to limit the trade rather than attempt to force outright abolition on an unwilling Sayyid Said, and in 1822 Captain Fairfax Moresby concluded a treaty with the Imam forbidding the sale of slaves to Christians. Although the Moresby Treaty proved ineffective, since Sayyid Said's actual control on the East African coast was tenuous at best, the British government had committed its power in support of the Imam, who could then attempt to reassert his claim to East Africa. Thus, the Moresby Treaty not only launched Sayyid Said into Africa, but as on the West Africa coast, British commitment to abolition was soon followed by direct British intervention.

By 1836 Sayyid Said had established his control in the islands and towns scattered along a thousand miles of the East African coast, had made Zanzibar his capital, and had proclaimed himself sultan. Peace and stability returned to East Africa. Clove plantations were introduced on Zanzibar Island, and trade, particularly the slave trade, expanded with capital supplied by Indian merchants who financed the Arab-led caravans that penetrated to the central African lakes in the interior. Having secured East Africa with British acquiescence, Sayyid Said could hardly ignore increasing British insistence that the slave trade be curtailed, despite the great opposition of his subjects and the prospect of financial loss. Therefore, he reluctantly agreed in 1845 to forbid the exportation of slaves from East Africa; but although he signed a treaty with Captain Atkins Hamerton, British consul in Zanzibar, the sultan could not enforce his decrees. Like its predecessor, the Hamerton Treaty proved ineffective. British naval patrols valiantly sought to check the numerous slave dhows that sailed between Africa and

Asia with even less success than the West African squadron had.

At first the British were content to trust in the naval patrols. However, the failure of the patrols and the vivid descriptions of the slave trade in the interior by the missionary-explorer David Livingstone combined to provide new impetus to the abolitionist movement at a time when it no longer seemed necessary in West Africa. In 1871 Parliament concluded that only complete prohibition would end the East African trade, and Sir Henry Bartle Frere, the former governor of Bombay, arrived in Zanzibar in 1873 to gain the agreement of Sayyid Said's successor, Sultan Barghash. The sultan refused. He knew that not only would the abolition of the slave trade deprive many of his subjects of their livelihood but also that it would result in the disappearance of slavery itself, since the birth rate among slaves was far below their mortality rate. Unable to achieve abolition by persuasion, the British resorted to force. Sir John Kirk, the British consul at Zanzibar, threatened to blockade Zanzibar, and the sultan surrendered. The slave trade was made illegal, the slave markets were closed, and the altar of the Universities Mission Cathedral Church was erected on the site of the whipping post, a symbol of the trade. Although the slave trade continued surreptitiously, it dwindled to insignificance by the end of the century.

The abolition of the slave trade did not go unopposed. The Swahili traders first tried to march the slaves northward along the coast for sale in Somaliland until prevented by the British patrols. Then the slavers at Kilwa plotted rebellion against Sultan Barghash, but the disturbances were curbed by ships and crews of the Royal Navy. Ironically, abolition drew Barghash and the British closer together. Without the Sultan, the abolition of the slave trade could only have been accomplished by direct British intervention. Without the British, Barghash would probably have been overthrown. By supporting the sultan's authority on the mainland, by training his army, and by reforming his administration, the British hoped to avoid direct rule in East Africa. There were contradictions inherent in this policy, however, since the British commitment in East Africa increased at the same time that Britain disclaimed any intention of acquiring an East African empire.

So long as no other European power challenged British influence at Zanzibar, this policy was brilliantly executed by Sir John Kirk, who had won the confidence and friendship of Sultan Barghash. By 1883 the Sultan, working in close cooperation with Kirk, had firmly established his authority all along the coast. But in the interior Barghash controlled only a few isolated outposts on the way to the lakes of equatorial Africa, where the great quest for the Nile sources had aroused the interest of England and Europe. The European explorers who reached the hinterland soon discovered that the sultan of Zanzibar did not, in fact, rule in the interior. Although Kirk at Zanzibar and the British Foreign Office in London might look upon East Africa as a sheltered preserve, protected by the nominal authority of the sultan, other powers, both Asian and European, were not willing to let the green hills of East Africa continue to be maintained only for the interests of a wiley Arab and a perfidious John Bull.

The literate public of England became captivated by the greatest geographical riddle of the latter half of the nineteenth century—the source of the Nile. The Nile quest was as old as antiquity. The Pharaohs, Herodotus, the Emperor Nero, scholars of the Middle Ages, and even Portuguese Jesuits had sought to find the "coy fountains" from which the Nile supposedly sprang. The explorations of James Bruce to the source of the Blue Nile in the eighteenth century had stirred peoples' imaginations. Reports and maps of German missionaries traveling in the interior of East Africa stimulated Richard Francis Burton and John Hanning Speke to set out from Zanzibar in 1856 to ascertain whether the mysterious Sea of Ujiji was in fact the Nile source. It was not. The Sea of Ujiji, or Lake Tanganyika as it became known, was found to have no outlet. But during the return march, John Hanning Speke discovered Lake Victoria to the north, which he declared the source of the Nile. Speke's discovery ignited a violent controversy, which was not completely resolved until the trans-African explorations of Henry Morton Stanley from 1874 to 1877. Speke, of course, was correct, but until Stanley conclusively proved that Lake Victoria was a single lake and the source of the Nile and that the Lualaba, or Congo, was a separate river and not part of the Nile system, the controversy raged in England, focusing the attention of the British public on the interior of Africa for twenty years. In succession, John Speke, Samuel Baker, David Livingstone, and finally Henry Morton Stanley, not to mention a host of lesser explorers, searched for the source of the Nile, providing tantalizing information to feed the fires of geographical speculation in England and for the first time opening the interior of East and equatorial Africa to a curious Europe. All the explorers wrote of their travels, and their accounts were widely read for the mixture of adventure, scientific discovery, and description of strange peoples. The Nile quest resulted in the explorations that opened the interior to the partitioners of Africa. By 1880 the way to the heart of Africa was known, although few followed the explorers there. Only in South Africa had Europeans come with the intention to conquer and control.

EUROPEANS IN
SOUTH AFRICA

At the end of the sixteenth century the Portuguese monopoly of the Indian trade was challenged by English and Dutch merchants, who hesitantly ventured into Eastern waters. Since their goal was to reach the East Indies, neither the British nor the Dutch ever displayed much interest in East African ports. Thus, the Cape of Good Hope became the last landfall for Dutch and English captains bound for the Orient. English interest, however, soon shifted to India. Since the seaway to India swung south of the hazardous coasts of southern Africa, British ships bound there rarely called at the Cape. The Dutch East India Company, however, sent Jan Van Riebeek to Table Bay, the harbor at Cape Town, in 1652 to establish a revictualing station. Unfortunately, Van Riebeek was unable to grow or to acquire by barter from the indigenous Khoikhoi population sufficient food to supply all the visiting ships; as a result, the company began to offer land grants to settlers from Holland in the hope of stimulating food production. Slowly the population of the settlement increased, and by the beginning of the eighteenth century there were sixteen hundred free burghers.

Thereafter immigration from Europe steadily declined as slaves were imported from West Africa in increasing numbers. Since slave labor was three times cheaper and more manageable than European farmhands, more white immigrants were not encouraged by the settlers or the Dutch East India Company. The free burgher population grew by natural increase rather than through immigration. Moreover, as the decades passed, the institution of slavery was not only accepted as the proper relationship between white and black men, but it was regarded as necessary to the colony's economy. The slave population, due to importation and internal increase, soon came to outnumber the free burghers. The settlers' links with Europe withered away, and they came to rely on slaves to meet their labor requirements.

Throughout the eighteenth century a slow but steady stream of colonists moved away from Cape Town and developed a pastoral economy in the hinterland, which was not unlike that of their black neighbors. Precipitated both by economic necessity and a desire to escape Company rule, this dispersion could not be stopped, although the Company opposed it. Not surprisingly, these Boers, as the migrants came to be called, were difficult people to govern, and the Company's failure to check their movements produced only contempt for its authority. In the end, the Company was reluctantly forced to extend its control into the interior, setting a pattern that was to be followed for over a century by successive authorities at the Cape. On the expanding frontiers of the colony, a distinct Boer culture developed, the product of a European heritage shaped by an African environment. Despite this expansion and the presence among the colonists of a sprinkling of English, Danish, and French Huguenot settlers, the character of the colony remained predominantly Dutch. Dutch was the language of the colony, and when infused with elements from French, German, English, and African languages, South African Dutch gradually evolved into the Afrikaans language of today. The inevitable social intercourse, intermarriage, the pervasive influence and popularity of the Dutch Reformed Church, which was Calvinist in theology and fundamentalist in practice, and isolation from the rapid and profound changes in seventeenth- and eighteenth-century Europe helped create a distinctive, homogeneous, white settler community at the Cape. At the end of the eighteenth century, however, this homogeneity was threatened first by the Bantu, sometimes called Kaffirs, and then by the British, who changed dramatically the cultural unity and demographic balance of the colony.

The first appearance of the Bantu in South Africa remains uncertain; they are believed to have been living south of the Limpopo River at the end of the first millennium. By 1800 the two principal divisions, the Nguni and Sotho-Tswana, had established numerous independent chieftaincies. Among them were the Xhosa, who pressed westward to the Great Fish River on the eastern border of the Cape Colony, where the river formed an uncertain frontier between the rapidly expanding Boer and Bantu societies. The clash of cultures and the competition for grazing land soon led to open disputes all along the frontier, which quickly developed into a succession of Kaffir Wars.

The British came to Cape Colony as the result of the wars of the French Revolution. As Britain's Indian and Oriental empire expanded during the eighteenth century, the Cape took on a strategic significance hitherto ignored, and when that empire was threatened by war with the French, the sea route to the East had to be secured. Consequently, the British occupied the Cape, and this occupation was made permanent by the Peace of Vienna in 1815. The relationship between the British and the Boers was at first simply that of ruler and ruled, but the arrival of

British settlers introduced a distinct and dynamic element into South African society that prevented the assimilation of either group by the other. At first the British and Boers found that they possessed many common sentiments which allowed for cooperation and friendship. In fact, cooperation between the British and the Dutch might well have grown into confidence and acceptance, if it had not been for their different attitudes toward and treatment of the black South Africans.

In South Africa the abolitionists were principally the British missionaries who preached a concept of human equality before God that was repugnant to the Boers, whose religious, economic, and social attitudes were based on a belief in the inferiority of the black Africans, which was ordained by God and justified his servile status. The abolition of slavery in the British Empire in 1833 coincided with an active policy of Anglicization in all branches of the colonial government and in the schools, which seemed to threaten the language, customs, and traditions of the Boers. Thus, in the mid-1830s, the frustrated and land-hungry Boers began to look, as they had done before, beyond the boundaries of the colony for the freedom they required to preserve their traditional way of life. The Great Trek into the interior of South Africa soon followed.

The Nguni-speaking Bantu had inhabited Zululand and Natal since at least the sixteenth century. There on the fertile grasslands between the Drakensberg Mountains and the Indian Ocean the Bantu population rapidly increased, land became scarce, and intertribal warfare intensified at the end of the eighteenth century. During this time of turmoil, Shaka, the son of the chief of a small Nguni tribe known as the Zulu, began to train his followers in new methods of warfare. By 1818 he had become the dominant power in what became Zululand. Introducing the concept of total war, Shaka's victorious armies swept all before them, precipitating the dispersal of hordes of refugees northward and westward. Destruction, upheaval, and death followed and transformed the rolling grasslands of the highveld into a deserted land open for Boer settlement.

Although the Great Trek did much to resolve, at least temporarily, the difficulties that the Boers had faced in the Cape Colony, it also created more problems for the British government. On the one hand, the Boers were technically British subjects who owed allegiance to the Crown, which was ultimately responsible for them, and yet the British government was reluctant to incur the great expense of administering the vast and unknown lands into which the Boers had fled. On the other hand, if the Boers were left alone to create their own independent states, the hinterland would be open for another European power to gain influence in southern Africa, jeopardizing the British position at the Cape and endangering the route to India. Moreover, since the Boers regarded the Bantu with implacable hostility and coveted their land and labor with self-righteous desire, the inevitable conflicts would keep the interior in confusion, adding expense to the British Treasury and resulting in insecurity about British strategy. To abandon the hinterland was strategically unthinkable. To control the frontier was financially inadmissable. The dilemmas of British rule in South Africa could not easily be resolved, and between 1836 and 1899 British policy vacillated wildly from abandoning the interior, to control by confederation, to direct rule. Ultimately, this erratic course alienated all parties in South Africa and led to a diminution of British influence.

Thus, in South Africa, as in other areas of Africa in this period, the British could not resolve the deep and fundamental conflict at home between economy of government expenditure and the demands of the humanitarians and of an expanding imperial frontier.

ATTITUDES
TOWARD
IMPERIALISM

Dramatic shifts in British policy in Africa precluded any coherent or conscious attempt to build an African empire, although there were numerous and influential advocates of colonization in nineteenth-century Britain. Some argued that colonial settlement was essential to solve domestic difficulties in Britain and that colonies would act as a safety valve for the problem of overpopulation or in the event of a popular insurrection. British reformers were closely allied and, in fact, were frequently members of special interest groups that had strong commitments in Africa, such as the abolitionists, the missionaries, the explorers, and the merchants. The ideas of the reformers and the special interests of the philanthropists and traders were pervasive and powerful but were not strong enough to command government policy. In reality their influence was limited and uneven. Throughout the nineteenth century Britain underwent a sweeping industrialization characterized at home by low taxation, limited public expenditure, and laissez faire, and abroad by free trade. Confident in her industrial and maritime supremacy, free trade became not only profitable, but an established creed in which the colonies were regarded as an unwanted financial burden. Thus, while the British Treasury constantly urged retrenchment, the conflicting interest groups encouraged the extension of imperial authority into the hinterland. The confusing British policies in Africa resulting from these contradictory objectives satisfied neither party, burdened the imperial taxpayer, and baffled historians.

The countries of continental Europe were even more uninterested in colonial expansion than was England. Abolition of the slave trade never appealed to the French as it did to the English. French explorers were as intrepid as their English counterparts but were fewer and less influential. The idea of overseas settlement by Frenchmen was never regarded as a positive solution to domestic problems. There were, of course, local traders in West Africa, such as Victor Régis, who had the support of sectional interests. But prestige for the monarchy and glory for the army appeared more important in sending France into Africa than trade, until imperial folly in Algeria checked such frivolous ambitions.

The Germans and Italians were even less interested than the French. Both were too concerned with the great struggle for unification and were too involved in the internal constitutional and social conflicts that followed to seek an overseas empire. To be sure, European expansion in Africa did occur during the first three-quarters of the nineteenth century. But the new outposts were acquired reluctantly, more as the result of the sheer momentum of past colonial policies, which met little political or geographical resistance in Africa, than of any new colonial objectives. Nevertheless, these outposts on the periphery of Africa constituted an informal empire that kept Europe committed in Africa at a time when Europeans were more absorbed with internal problems than with overseas expansion. They laid the foundations for expansion that was to occur when shifts in the European balance of power and new ideologies appeared, turning the attention of Europeans outward to the world beyond and to the brooding continent of Africa.

Chapter 3

Partition
and Pacification

During three centuries of contact with Africa, the European powers had been content, except in South Africa, to restrict their holdings to a handful of scattered trading stations along the coasts, the control of which passed from one country to another as the strength of each waxed or waned in Europe. Although in the nineteenth century European explorers finally penetrated the interior and opened the enormous hinterland of Africa, no European government rushed to follow in their footsteps. Stimulated by the evangelism and humanitarianism produced by the crusade against the slave trade, missionaries began to work out from the coastal enclaves, but they never regarded themselves as agents of the home governments. In fact, until the European acquisition of Africa, the missionaries argued that, given proper training, the Africans themselves were the best equipped to carry Christianity among the African peoples. Even the commercial interests were reluctant to see the extension of European control. Along the coast, particularly in West Africa, an equilibrium existed between European traders and African middlemen. The more astute merchants realized that intervention, occupation, and rule by any single European power would not necessarily benefit them. These traders supported the doc-

᠁ine of free trade, satisfied to derive reasonable gain for the many, rather than monopoly profits for the few. Thus, on the threshold of the partition of Africa, a balance of influence existed among the Europeans themselves and, except in South Africa, an equilibrium was maintained between the European and African societies. Yet there were signs that this equilibrium was beginning to break down. The presence of missionaries, merchants, explorers, and soldiers had cleared the way for the expansion of Europe into Africa. From these contacts the Africans had been exposed to and had absorbed Western technology and organization. When adapted to African societies and employed by the Africans in pursuit of their own interests, these dynamic European devices tended to upset the balance of influence between Europeans and Africans. To be sure, nothing in history is inevitable until it occurs. Yet within less than twenty years the African continent was conquered and divided amid rising nationalist feeling at home and increasing belligerency among Europeans abroad. The explanations for this phenomenon are nearly as unsatisfactory as they are numerous. The interpretations are as controversial as they are doctrinaire. The misconceptions are as enduring as they are erroneous. To scholar and student alike, the search for an understanding of this dynamic period, which dramatically altered the future of the vast African continent, holds out an intellectual challenge more than equal to the intellectual rewards.

 The nineteenth century was an age of European expansion in knowledge as well as in territory. The foundations of science laid down in the seventeenth and eighteenth centuries permitted the construction of an ever-enlarging body of scientific learning. The practical application of this learning produced a new technology to meet the insatiable demands of expanding industry, its products provided Europeans with undreamed of power and more time for intellectual inquiry and political participation. Even Christianity expanded. Under assault by secular philosophy and scientific thought, the Church lost its former hold on men's minds at home and sought to make good its

losses by seeking new recruits overseas. Stimu.
an outburst of evangelism, Christian missionar..
out not only to convert the heathens, but to acco.
plish social and scientific objectives as well. Thus,
while David Livingstone was more interested in exploration than in conversion, in abolition of the slave
trade than in evangelism, his writings not only focused
British attention on Africa, but also his personal experiences inspired many to leave Europe to spread the
word of Christ in Africa.

②The expansion of knowledge, the triumphs of science and technology, and the improvement in the
standard of living produced a cultural self-confidence
in Europe that found popular and political expression
in nationalism. Technological superiority was often
confused with national superiority, and it helped create a rationale for conquering supposedly less cultured
peoples and an unswerving confidence in the benefits
of European rule for them. As a result, the technological advances of the industrial revolution helped upset
the balance of power between Europe and Africa.

③ ✱ Cultural self-confidence was characteristic of all the
European powers, but particularly of Germany, who,
after the victories of the Franco-Prussian War of 1870,
became the strongest continental power. Unified by
blood and iron, the military monarchy ruled in a
Germany where any threat of uprising was alleviated
by the vision of an unlimited, if ill-defined, future in
which colonialism seemed, for the first time, a viable
solution to Germany's problems. Like the great nations of Europe, Germany argued that she, too, must
acquire colonies overseas in order to establish protected
markets for German industry, and that she too had a
responsibility to provide enlightened administration
and to promote economic progress for backward peoples. Like space exploration is for the United States
and Russia today, the acquisition of colonies was for
Germany a symbol of prestige and of her investiture
as a great power. By the last quarter of the nineteenth
century German enthusiasm for overseas expansion
was irrepressible. Organizations like the German Colonial League (Gesellschaft für Deutsche Kolonisa-

on) were characterized by romantic chauvinism and presented a vociferous mixture of economic, geographical, and naval interests.

Germany was not alone in looking beyond Europe er 1870. In 1871 the preeminent position of France in Europe had come to an end. Many Frenchmen began to look overseas for the greatness that had vanished in Europe. They hoped to regenerate France and to regain in Africa and Asia what they had lost in Alsace-Lorraine. By 1876 over 300,000 Europeans, mostly French, had emigrated to Algeria, where French farmers acquired new vineyards to replace those they had lost in Europe. French intellectuals—journalists, scholars, civil servants, and army officers—began to write on colonial questions. Most argued that colonies were proof of a national vitality that would result in economic gain. Not only would the acquisition of new territories broaden man's intellectual horizons, but also it would provide raw materials for French factories, markets for French manufactured products, and investments for French capital. What Frenchmen could resist the combination of scientific inquiry, intellectual enterprise, and profits? The colonial challenge was for the brave and the bold, the men of the future who were not content to remain in their appointed stations in a Europe where international peace and internal quiescence limited individual initiative.

Much the same attitude prevailed among colonial enthusiasts in England, marked, however, by growing apprehension as the confidence of the mid-century British gave way to the hesitancies of the late Victorians. Throughout the first three-quarters of the nineteenth century Great Britain's worldwide naval and commercial supremacy had remained unquestioned. Thereafter, the British had to face, for the first time, very real competition from the United States and from continental Europe, particularly from the newly unified nation-states. Perhaps, after all, colonies might not be an unwanted financial burden for the mother country, but rather economic and human assets with which to meet the challenge from land-based powers like Germany, Russia, and the United States. The argument that if territory were not claimed now it would be lost for future needs became a convincing one to many Englishmen who previously did not favor the expansion of the British Empire. Like the advocates of colonialism in France, British imperialists argued that colonies were an economic benefit. They did so, however, for opposite reasons from their continental counterparts. Rather than regard the colonies as protected markets, assured sources of raw materials, and isolated opportunities for investment, some Englishmen believed that the empire represented a powerful free-trade union, which would act as a counterweight to the protectionism of the continental European powers. Others still retained the old belief that colonies were an outlet for overpopulation and consequently, a remedy for poverty at home. A new, more pervasive, mood also captured the minds and imagination of many Englishmen: the growing emphasis on "bigness" in industry and society carried over into a desire for expansion to gain prestige for the empire. To many, particularly the British working class, this sentiment was expressed in jingoist, flag-waving assertions of British power. Others believed that it was the duty of an advanced civilization such as Britain to guide backward peoples out of darkness. Taking on trusteeship was the price of power, and prestige was the reward for carrying the torch of civilization into the unknown. Together these ideas created persuasive new arguments in favor of imperialism and a popular enthusiasm for empire in striking contrast to the parsimony of the Little Englanders and the pacificism of the Liberals. Imperialism became not only popular, but good politics.

The assumption and growing acceptance of the idea that overseas expansion was a characteristic of national greatness did not cause the partition of Africa; it only helped make the scramble possible. So, too, did the technological gap between Europe and Africa. By the last quarter of the nineteenth century scientific and technological advances not only made partition possible, but proved decisive in the subsequent conquest and occupation of the African continent. Since the discovery of quinine, the malarial areas of tropical Africa were no longer a white man's grave. The steamship revolutionized maritime trade and naval strategy, obliterating previously formidable distances, opening precarious ports of call, and carrying enormous human and material cargos. The locomotive accomplished on land what the steamship achieved on the high seas, and remote hinterlands could now be exposed to large numbers of intruders, be they soldiers, traders, or settlers. The disparity between African and European technology was even greater in the development of weapons. The invention of repeating rifles and automatic weapons, such as the Maxim gun, invested the Europeans with an enormous military superiority. Although Africans obtained considerable numbers of modern rifles, they never acquired enough quick-firing guns to oppose the Europeans effectively.

If European imperialism in Africa became acceptable in the closing decades of the nineteenth century and European technological superiority made that imperialism possible, it was the political weakness of the traditional African states vis-à-vis the European nation-states that made the European conquest a reality. Many African states fought a valiant, if futile, struggle against European invasion, and a long period of resistance did, in fact, follow the initial European conquest in many parts of Africa. Some African states sought to use the Europeans for their own purposes. But traditional political institutions generally failed to meet the European challenge. The inequality between the administrative, bureaucratic, and diplomatic resources of the greatest African state and even the weakest European colonial power was too large for African authorities to maintain their independence without enlisting the aid of a rival European nation; and almost without exception, and despite political and economic conflicts in Europe, the European powers consistently supported one another when faced by a strong state in Africa. Everywhere thrown on the defensive, African polities certainly influenced and conditioned the scramble and frequently forced the

Europeans to compromise their objectives, but the European powers nevertheless determined the partition, occupation, and pacification of Africa.

THE SCRAMBLE
BEGINS

Many scholars have sought to provide a comprehensive interpretation of the partition of Africa. Unhappily, no such single explanation has proven completely applicable to the varied events of this period. Indeed, the complexities of the scramble appear to defy any general, comprehensive interpretation, for the great diversity of Africa and its peoples and the inextricable interests and motives of the European powers preclude any single sweeping theory to explain the partition in every region of the continent. In the end a more meaningful and accurate understanding of the partition can be best achieved by regarding the scramble as a series of interconnected events, which were conditioned by different patterns of human motivation and behavior in each of the disparate regions of Africa.

There were hesitant beginnings to the partition of Africa in the 1870s. The discovery of diamonds in South Africa in 1869 provided the incentive and capital for a large influx of Europeans, who ultimately spilled across the Limpopo River into Central Africa. The opening of the Suez Canal in the same year, made possible by the development of the steamship, not only made the East African coast more accessible, but also soon became the great pivotal point in British imperial strategy; British interest shifted to Cairo with repercussions as far south as the great lakes of equatorial Africa and as far west as Wadai and Lake Chad. In 1881 the French reluctantly extended their control over Tunis; like the British in Egypt, Zanzibar, and Turkey, the French had hoped to maintain their influence by supporting the government of the Bey, the Tunisian ruler, and to avoid annexation. Like the British, the French discovered to their dismay that financial and diplomatic manipulation was insufficient to maintain French influence against indigenous resistance to their interference. They either had to control Tunis or leave her to the Italians, who had also hoped to acquire her. The French chose to control Tunis, and the Italian reaction to the French seizure was to turn against the monarchy rather than to clamor for alternative territory in Africa. The occupation of Tunis, therefore, did not precipitate or signal the beginning of the scramble for Africa. The partition of Africa required greater stimuli than the discovery of diamonds in South Africa or political intrigue on the Mediterranean littoral. The partitioners did not have long to wait.

On the morning of September 13, 1882, the British army under the command of General Sir Garnet Wolseley assaulted the entrenchment of the Egyptian forces at Tell el-Kebir in an effort to preserve British influence in Egypt and the Suez Canal. The French had remained aloof from an invitation to join the British attack and thereafter sulked at a missed opportunity to advance French interests on the Nile. Spearheaded by the Scots of the Highland Brigade, the British troops carried the Egyptian fortifications in twenty minutes and within the hour had routed the Egyptian forces. Tell el-Kebir was a complete and decisive British victory. Not only had the Egyptian army been destroyed, but a somewhat muddled British government found itself in sole control of Cairo. The British occupied Egypt with great reluctance, and they had sought to maintain their influence at Cairo by supporting the khedival, or Turkish viceregal, government, not by doing away with it. Like the French in Tunisia, the British had failed.

The Khedive Ismail, in his valiant attempts to modernize and expand his empire, drove Egypt into bankruptcy in 1876 by his profligate spending. Britain and France intervened and assumed control of Egyptian finances. Intervention, however, produced a strong reaction. Led by Colonel Ahmad Arabi Pasha, a nationalist uprising swept through Egypt destroying European property and lives and disrupting European control until the British army crushed the nationalists and occupied the country.

British statesmen intended the occupation to be temporary, at best for a few months, at worst for a few years. They had invaded Egypt to protect European financial interests, to restore European political influence, and to secure the Suez Canal, the life line to Britain's Oriental empire. When these objectives were achieved, the British were prepared to depart. No one envisaged a long occupation, and no one imagined that the British presence on the shores of the Mediterranean Sea would result in British commitments in tropical Africa. To contemporaries, the British occupation of Egypt appeared to have no relation to Africa south of the Sahara. British officials refused to support the Egyptians in the Sudan and, comforted by the thought they would soon be leaving, assured the European powers that they had no territorial ambitions elsewhere on the African continent. The partition of Africa seemed the least likely outcome of the occupation. Yet even before Britain imposed its rule on Egypt, Henry Morton Stanley, the famous explorer and journalist, began to lay claims to the south bank of the Congo on behalf of his employer, King Leopold II of Belgium, while Savorgnan de Brazza had already concluded treaties on the north bank for France.

Leopold II had always wanted a colony. In 1876 he founded the International African Association (Association Internationale de Congo), and between 1878 and 1879 he dabbled in East African schemes. After Stanley had descended the Congo River in 1877, thereby opening the great basin of that river, the king's interests turned increasingly to the Congo. In 1879 Stanley returned to the Congo as King Leopold's representative to establish stations on the river for the Committee for the Study of the Upper Congo (Comité d'Etudes du Haut-Congo), which Leopold had created to further his growing interest in the region. Leopold had virtually no support in Belgium for colonization, and the penny-pinching burghers of Brussels were not inclined to embark on expensive schemes of colonization with little prospect of profit or prestige. Nevertheless, Leopold engendered sympathy in Europe and the United States by appealing to humanitarian sentiment against the slave trade, by stimulating geographical curiosity, and by calling attention to the economic potential of tropical products. By skill-ful diplomacy, intrigue, and the judicious use of his own wealth, he was determined to establish himself in Africa. During the next five years Stanley worked as-siduously for the king to negotiate treaties with the Africans, to build stations, and to construct lines of communication a thousand miles up the river to Stan-ley Falls. He was not alone.

In 1880 Savorgnan de Brazza arrived on his second expedition to Gabon. He traveled up the Ogowe River, passed over the height of land, and marched down to the Congo River where he signed a treaty in September 1880 with Makoko, chief of the Bateke, in which Ma-koko ceded his territory to France. Brazza established a small post under a Senegalese sergeant on the site of the future city of Brazzaville and raised the French flag. Nearly a year later, Stanley returned and found himself forestalled. Making the best of a bad job, he claimed the south bank for Leopold and his Interna-tional Association of the Congo, which had replaced the Committee for the Study of the Upper Congo, and which was neither international nor an association, but an instrument and a screen for the king's activi-ties. Brazza returned to France to a hero's welcome in June 1882, just two months before the British victory at Tell el-Kebir. Two months after the British occu-pation of Egypt, in November 1882, the French Chamber ratified Brazza's treaty with Makoko and appropriated 3.5 million francs to organize the new territory. In April 1883 French protectorates were declared over Contonou and Porto-Novo on the coast of West Africa. With a surge of patriotic fervor this press into Africa overcame the past reluctance for empire of French legislators, local economic groups, and statesmen; almost overnight it captivated the im-agination and interests of the French public. Until then, imperial adventures had brought only humilia-tion and expense. Now the French were promised pres-tige and riches. Having failed to act on the Nile, France could not ignore the Congo. Although Brazza-ville could not compensate for Cairo nor could Con-tonou overcome the disgrace of indecision in Egypt, nevertheless, the Makoko Treaty put France squarely on the map of interior equatorial Africa, and the British victory in Egypt had been a decisive factor in France's decision. The partition of Africa was beginning.

Unwilling to be left behind, Leopold had not been idle. Brazza's intervention had dramatically demonstrated that Leopold could not maintain his trading stations in the Congo against foreign competition without the protective mantle of sovereignty. Faced by the power of France and Portugal, who had claims in the Congo, the King was now forced to seek more actively sovereign rights for what had been ostensibly a scientific and commercial association. To be sure, Stanley had momentarily countered the French threat north of the Congo River by laying claim to the south bank, but Portuguese rights to the mouth of the Congo presented a more immediate danger to Leopold's presence in the Congo basin. The Portuguese claims were ancient, going back to the first contacts between Portugal and the Kingdom of the Kongo in the fifteenth century. Thereafter, they languished—paper rights of past greatness. But no empire, however feeble or inefficient, could permit its claims to vanish by default. In fact, the very antiquity of Portuguese rights seemed to demand their vigorous defense. Portugal did not have to act alone. Alarmed by the aggressive activities of Leopold and Brazza, Great Britain sought to close the mouth of the Congo and thereby neutralize the interior. In February 1884 Britain recognized Portuguese claims in the Congo by the Anglo-Portuguese Agreement.

The Anglo-Portuguese Treaty was in trouble from the start. Portugal was Catholic and long the purveyor of slaves. British Protestant missionaries and humanitarians were shocked by the association of Liberal Britain with the corrupt and decaying Portuguese empire. Moreover, British commercial interests were equally furious that the England of free trade should support the narrow protectionism of Portugal. And, of course, cajoling, intriguing, and supporting the opposition to the Treaty was King Leopold, who worked frantically to save his claims upriver by ensuring the vital access to the sea. By skillful diplomacy and clever propaganda he created the myth that only his International African Association could keep the French and Portuguese protectionist powers out of the Congo while bringing civilization to darkest Africa. His propaganda did indeed rally support for Leopold both in Britain and elsewhere, but it also exacerbated old rivalries, stimulated national fears, and stirred up suspicion in the chancelleries of Europe. Only in an atmosphere of tension, jealousy, and chauvinism could Leopold be the least threat to the contending interests in the Congo of the other powers.

Suddenly, in the midst of this diplomacy of apprehension, a new and awesome competitor appeared—Germany. In 1883 Bismarck, the Chancellor of Germany, decided that Germany needed colonies. His motives still remain unclear but appear to have been generated by Germany's position in Europe and Bismarck's position in Germany more than by any local African factors or German economic interests. In Africa, Bismarck could utilize German diplomacy to support French dreams against British pretensions and, hopefully, thereby take the first step toward a Franco-German reconciliation, which the occupation of Alsace-Lorraine had hitherto made impossible. In Africa, Bismarck could acquire colonies to stimulate patriotic feeling within Germany and, consequently, support for the empire and himself. Clearly, Bismarck's control of the German government was too authoritarian to permit the handful of German merchants in Africa or even the more powerful German Colonial League to dictate policy, but if they profited from colonies abroad, they would surely support the Chancellor at home.

Once he was determined to seize colonies, Bismarck set out to collect them swiftly and ruthlessly. In a year and a half, between 1884 and 1885, Germany acquired extensive regions in South-West Africa, Togoland, the Cameroons, and East Africa. Until the German annexations the European powers had not yet overcome their hesitancy to precipitate a land rush in tropical Africa. The British were particularly reluctant to take on new commitments in Africa, and their diplomacy was aimed more at preventing the partition of Africa than at encouraging it. The French had been aggressive, but the first flush of empire soon wore off and was followed by a hangover of hesitancy. By this time Leopold could hardly contain his desire for the Congo, but his weak position in Europe and his limited resources in Africa forced him to remain in the shadows until his diplomacy and luck illuminated the way to sovereignty in equatorial Africa. Portugal did not seem to count.

A PAUSE IN THE SCRAMBLE German intervention resolved all uncertainty. Not only did Bismarck seize territory on both sides of the African continent, but he joined with France in October 1884 to invite twelve other states to a conference in Berlin to discuss free trade in the Congo basin, freedom of navigation on the Niger and the Congo rivers, and the requirements for international recognition of European occupation in Africa. The conference opened in November 1884. It passed an act incorporating vague and pious pronouncements regarding the slave trade, free trade, and the ground rules for occupation. In practice they were to prove largely ineffectual. Of greater consequence was the recognition by the powers of King Leopold's claims to the Congo, but even this international investiture was a foregone conclusion, since France, Germany, and the United States had individually recognized the sovereignty of Leopold's International African Association in the Congo before the opening of the conference. The real importance of the Berlin Conference for the partition of Africa, however, was neither the Berlin Act, which it produced, nor Leopold's rule in the Congo, which it sanctioned, but the realization that partition was now practicable. When the Berlin Conference ended in February 1885, the scramble for Africa could have been in full swing.

Once the rules for the partition were agreed upon, the contestants did not immediately take advantage of the opportunities those rules presented. Bismarck had taken much in a short time. His ambitions in Africa seemed to be satisfied. In addition, Bismarck required British support for Austria against Russia in the Balkans more than he needed British animosity in Africa. Germany made no new acquisitions in Africa, confining herself in later years to expanding those colonies acquired between 1884 and 1885. Leopold, of course, had the Congo; because of financial difficulties he could hardly claim more, at least for the moment.

France had been the most energetic imperialist, but in March 1885 Jules Ferry, the leading architect of French colonialism, fell from power. It was another five years before the French colonial movement succeeded in overcoming the obstinate and vocal opposition to French overseas expansion that had been momentarily stilled during the heady days of the Makoko Treaty. In the meantime, the French officers who sought the military glory in Africa that they could not win in Europe were checked, if not defeated, by the heroic defense of the Africans—Samori and others in the Sudan, King Gele and Behanzin in Dahomey, and later Rabih Zubayr in the Chad.

The British were no more imminently aggressive than their rivals. Bechuanaland in southern Africa had been annexed in 1885 to counter the Germans in South-West Africa and the Boers in the Transvaal, but thereafter in southern Africa the initiative was in the hands of individuals from the Cape Colony whose avaricious and patriotic motives did not immediately commit the imperial government south of the Zambezi. But here the British had no serious European rivals. True, the Portuguese after 1886 had sought to revive their claims to the interior of Central Africa linking Angola and Mozambique, but neither Portuguese pride nor manipulation could overcome British power. That power was represented not so much by the imperial government as by a private individual— Cecil John Rhodes.

Cecil Rhodes had come to Africa for his health and had drifted to the diamond fields, where, by buying up small bankrupt claims, he formed De Beers Consolidated Mines, Limited, and became a very wealthy man. He did not regard money as an end in itself, but rather as a means to extend British control into Central Africa. Rhodes' interest in Central Africa was stimulated by the discovery of gold in the Transvaal, and he predicted that additional gold reserves would be discovered north of the Limpopo River, producing a "Second Rand," which would attract British immigrants and create a new British state in the hinterland. Thereafter, neither Boer nor Bantu would be able to challenge British domination in southern Africa. Founding the British South Africa Company to spearhead the drive to the northern interior, Rhodes utilized his great wealth and political position as Prime Minister of the Cape Colony to secure Rhodesia and frustrate Portugal's claims to the interior. Only when a Portuguese expedition was sent into the Shire Highlands in 1889 did the British government, with strong support from Rhodes, directly intervene to prevent Portuguese acquisition of Malawi and clear the way for the formulation of British claims north of the Zambezi River. Having easily brushed aside their only European rival in southern Africa, the British had even less to fear from the indigenous people; by the 1890s the Bantu groups had been subdued. The conflict with the Boers, who counted for little in international relations, was a decade away. Thus, immediately after 1885 the scramble for Africa appeared to be in slow motion. The decisive factor in its acceleration was Egypt.

BRITAIN'S NILOTIC IMPERATIVE — In the autumn of 1888 the prime minister of Great Britain, Lord Salisbury, decided that the occupation of Egypt would have to become more permanent. The implications of this decision were far-reaching. It precipitated the second round in the scramble for Africa. Once the British determined to remain in Egypt, they were committed to its defense. Egypt is a desert that is made to bloom only by the waters that pour out of equatorial Africa and from the highlands of Ethiopia. No African peoples possessed the technological skills to interfere with the northward flow of the Nile waters. The European powers did. Thus, to protect Suez, that life line of empire, the British had to remain in Cairo. When they decided to take up permanent residence in Egypt, they had to defend the Nile waters, wherever they were, be it Khartoum, Lake Tana, Fashoda, or Uganda. The Berlin Conference may have presaged the partition of eastern Africa; Egypt made it inevitable.

The first threat to the Nile Valley came from Italy. In the great battle of Al-Gallabat between the Mahdists of the Sudan and the forces of King John of Ethiopia, the king was killed by a chance bullet and the Ethiopians routed.* The Mahdists marched all the way to Gondar before retiring due to the cold and disease in the hill country. Ethiopia was thrown into chaos by the rival factions competing for successions to the Crown of the Lion of Judah, King of Kings, and Emperor of all the Ethiopians. In this fluid situation Menelik, the king of Shoa, sought Italian support to consolidate his position as emperor. In May 1889 he signed the Treaty of Uccialli. To the Italians, Ethiopia had become a protectorate. To Menelik, it was merely an alliance. The premier of Italy, Francesco Crispi, an avowed imperialist, was prepared to re-create in Africa the grandeur of imperial Rome. The Treaty of Uccialli was followed by an Italian invasion, which, however, led to a disastrous defeat for the Italian army at the Battle of Aduwa in March 1896, ending for a generation Italian attempts to conquer Ethiopia. Meanwhile, so long as the Italians remained in the highlands, the British were happy to have someone keep Menelik busy and out of the Nile Valley. When the Italians proved more aggressive, however, and occupied Kassala below the Ethiopian escarpment, Lord Salisbury wasted no time in warning them to keep out of the Nile Valley. Deeply embroiled with Menelik, they agreed.

---

* The Mahdists were the followers of Muhammad Ahmad, who declared himself the Mahdi in 1881 and led his Sudanese supporters in revolt against Turko-Egyptian rule in the Sudan. In 1885 Khartoum was captured, and the Mahdi established the independent Mahdist state in the Sudan.

Having rid himself of the Italians, Salisbury next had to face the more powerful Germans. Although Bismarck had disclaimed any designs on the Central Africa lakes, his successors did not. The kaiser was particularly smitten with "equatorial madness," and Carl Peters, one of the most ambitious German imperialists, having eluded British naval patrols, reached the German enclave of Witu and raced inland to sign a treaty in 1890 with Mwanga, Kabaka, or king, of Buganda, who was situated on the shores of Lake Victoria, the enormous reservoir of the White Nile. Peters' movements did not go unnoticed. With the support of Sir William Mackinnon, a leading British advocate of imperialism and founder of the Imperial British East Africa Company, Salisbury struck a bargain with the Germans, the Anglo-German Agreement of 1890, which restricted the Germans to the southern shore of Lake Victoria in return for the island of Helgoland off the coast of Germany. The vital region north of Lake Victoria in Uganda was preserved for Britain. By 1890 the Nile sources seemed secure.

During the negotiations with the Germans in 1890 Salisbury was faced with a dilemma. He wanted to save Uganda and the Upper Nile for Britain. To do so, however, meant abandoning to the Germans the territory south and east of Lake Victoria between Lake Edward and Lake Tanganyika. Unfortunately, this triangular region formed a strategic link in the Cape-to-Cairo Railway, a scheme which had captured the imaginations of Britain's leading and most powerful imperialists—Mackinnon, Rhodes, and their supporters. Salisbury cared very little for an All-Red Route from Cape Town to Cairo, but he cared a great deal about the political support of those who wanted the railway.* How could he defend the Nile without losing the Cape-to-Cairo Railway and its proponents?

---

* In the late nineteenth century the idea of a chain of British possessions stretching from Cape Town to Cairo along the spine of Africa captivated the imagination of the British public. The idea was commonly referred to as the "All-Red Route," since the British empire was invariably colored in red on maps of Africa and of the world.

King Leopold supplied the answer. In a treaty with Sir William Mackinnon's Imperial British East Africa Company, which at that time was carrying British interests into the interior of East Africa, Leopold leased a corridor to the Company behind German East Africa, thereby providing the all-important link between Lake Tanganyika, which touched the British sphere in the south, and Lake Edward, whose shores met the British sphere in the north. Since Leopold never did anything for nothing, the price of that astute monarch's cooperation was the extension of his Congo Free State's sphere of influence to the Nile. Salisbury kept out the Germans but let in King Leopold.

In 1890 Salisbury did not regard King Leopold as a Nilotic rival. Like many other European statesmen, he seriously underestimated Leopold, for no sooner was the ink dry on the Mackinnon Treaty than the king began to make plans to march to the Nile. His forces reached the Upper Nile in 1892 and at Wadelai raised the blue banner with the golden star of the Congo Free State. The British were stunned. The Mackinnon Treaty was immediately repudiated, and Leopold was told in blunt terms to stay out of the Nile basin. Leopold might have resisted, but his forces had to retire before the Mahdists, and with the retreat of his troops King Leopold lost his principal weapon for negotiation.

FRENCH IMPERIALISM REVIVES

While Leopold's forces withdrew from the Nile, the French were on the move. Under the direction of Eugène Etienne, the undersecretary for the colonies in 1887 and from 1889 to 1892, the French colonial movement was revived. Employing the economic arguments of Jules Ferry, Etienne fashioned an aggressive and coordinated program for French imperialism in Africa. The colonial enthusiasm that he generated in France was reciprocated by the bronzed and heroic young cavalrymen in Africa, who were more concerned with checking Islam and winning personal glory by daring military exploits than with advancing French economic interests.

Thus, the French empire in the Western Sudan was

advanced less by French economic designs than by the impetuous and frequently insubordinate actions of military governors like Colonel Louis Archinard, whose activities French statesmen privately disapproved but could not publicly disavow. Archinard, for example, destroyed the Tucolor state of Ahmadu, occupied its capital, Segu, then Timbuktu, and finally drove the remnants of the Tucolor forces eastward into the Fulani empire of Sokoto. Similarly, political rather than economic factors moved the French to eliminate the empire of Samori Ture south of the upper Niger. If heroism had been sufficient, the French would have occupied the interior of West Africa in a few months. In fact, however, the resistance of African leaders like Ahmadu and Ture was determined enough to prolong the conquest for several years. But to these French officers, a hard-fought campaign, so long as it was won, was invariably more glorious than a peaceful promenade. In this pursuit of prestige, the French drive for the Nile was launched.

On January 20, 1893, the French hydrologist Victor Prompt delivered a paper entitled *"Soudan Nilotique"* before the Egyptian Institute in Paris. Prompt did not confine his remarks simply to Nile hydrology, however. He suggested that a dam constructed on the Upper Nile could destroy Egypt; that who controlled Fashoda, controlled Cairo. Prompt's lecture had a profound impact on the new undersecretary for the colonies, Theophile Delcassé. It was circulated among the French ministries at precisely the time when the British foreign secretary had peremptorily rebuffed a French offer to negotiate an agreement to withdraw the British from Egypt. Since the British refused to discuss the Egyptian question upon invitation, they had to be intimidated by the threat of interference in the Nile region. In May 1893 Prompt was summoned to the Elyseé Palace where, in private discussions among Sadi Carnot, president of the Republic, Commandant P. L. Monteil, the well-known French explorer, and Delcassé, the great French Fashoda expedition was born. Founded on the superficial speculations of Prompt, the intrigue of Delcassé, and the enthusiasm of President Carnot, the march to Fashoda began under the guise of the Monteil Mission. The only one who appeared reluctant was Commandant Monteil. He insisted upon obtaining the support of the Congo Free State, but King Leopold was in no hurry to help the French get to the Upper Nile before he did. His obstruction not only delayed the Monteil Mission, but it provided the opportunity for the new premier of France, Casimir-Perier, who strongly disapproved of the project, to terminate the mission.

Although frustrated in France, the Monteil Mission was not forgotten either by the men of the Pavillon de Flore, the French Colonial Ministry, or by officials in Whitehall, the British Foreign Office. British intelligence knew of the Monteil expedition; it required little imagination to guess its destination. Thus, the Liberals' foreign secretary, Lord Rosebery, was faced with the same problem as his Conservative predecessor, Lord Salisbury—how to keep European rivals out of the Nile Valley without actually occupying it. Salisbury had frightened off the Italians by threats and, with an assist from King Leopold, had bought off the Germans with Helgoland. Rosebery could obviously not bully France, and he certainly was not going to withdraw from Egypt. In desperation he turned to King Leopold. On May 12, 1894, the Anglo-Congolese Agreement was signed. It was, in essence, a revised version of the Mackinnon Treaty and leased to King Leopold on various terms the whole of the Upper Nile basin west of the river and south of Fashoda. The French were blocked but not, however, for long.

The French were indignant when they learned of the treaty, but that was to be expected. What was not foreseen was the violent reaction in Germany. In return for the loss of the Upper Nile the British received a corridor in Congolese territory behind German East Africa. The Tanganyika strip had been more an afterthought than a condition, a sop to the Cape-to-Cairo crowd. Unwilling to anger the Germans, Britain did nothing to support King Leopold. Deserted and thoroughly frightened by the veiled threats from Berlin,

Leopold gave way and abrogated the article ceding the Tanganyika corridor. Having given way to the Germans, the king could not refuse the French. On August 14, 1894, he signed an agreement with France, limiting his once vast lease to an insignificant enclave at Lado on the Nile. The way to Fashoda was free and clear.

PARTITION IN WEST AFRICA The failure of the Anglo-Congolese Agreement marks the beginning of the last great act of the partition in tropical Africa. The French advance across the Western Sudan was gaining momentum, and their final push toward the Nile was less than a year in the future. Along the coast of West Africa as well, the pace of partition was quickening as the economic forces, which had been gathering strength for over a decade, became increasingly intertwined with questions of prestige and strategy to compel the European governments to play a more active role in the interior. Although economic factors were more critical in this area than in most other regions of Africa, no single explanation for the scramble in West Africa can be isolated and universally applied throughout the area. Not only do the motives for European imperialism vary dramatically from place to place, but the particular primacy of any single reason is invariably obscured by the presence of important secondary considerations.

As in East and Central Africa, the British advance into Nigeria was led by a commercial concern—the African National Company. Unlike their campaigns in the Western Sudan and the Congo, the French advances along the Slave Coast and in the Niger basin were led by merchants from Marseilles and Rouen. Throughout the 1870s European coastal traders began to penetrate up the Niger River to the markets of the interior in an effort to by-pass the African middlemen and chiefs along the coast who had long controlled trade with the hinterland. This was an expensive and fiercely competitive operation, particularly when dealing with the powerful Fulani emirates of northern Nigeria, and resulted in the amalgamation of rival British firms under the brilliant direction of

Sir George Goldie, who undercut the French and German firms to establish a virtual monopoly on the river. In 1886 Goldie's African National Company became the Royal Niger Company under a royal charter permitting the Company to administer justice and to maintain order as well as to trade in the Niger interior. The French responded with political support for their faltering commercial concerns, and although the struggle for control never reached the intensity of the Nile quest, the race for Borgu between the French Captain Decoeur and Captain Lugard of the Royal Niger Company signaled another and more militant round in the contest for control of the lower Niger, which caused the British government to play a more active role than it had in the past.

Economic interests were of less importance to Britain's acquisition of Ashanti and Yorubaland than they had been on the Niger. Relations between the British and the Ashanti and the Yoruba had been conditioned by the British military victory over the Ashanti in 1874 and by the presence of Christian missionaries in Yorubaland. But the threat of French and German intervention in these two traditional British spheres of influence proved more decisive in the resolve of the British government to assert its authority than was the concern to protect any economic or humanitarian interests. After 1895, Joseph Chamberlain, the new and energetic British colonial secretary, had no intention of bargaining away deserts in West Africa for interests in eastern and southern Africa as Salisbury had done in 1890. Vigorously supporting British men of action in West Africa and stubbornly rejecting Salisbury's concessions in London, Chamberlain sanctioned an expedition to occupy Ashanti in 1896 and to consolidate British control in the hinterland of Sierra Leone; by 1897 he was determined to resist French encroachment into the lower Niger.

In 1898 the charter of the Royal Niger Company was terminated and the British government accepted the direct responsibility for defending the British sphere in northern Nigeria, which had proved too expensive for a private company whose monopolistic practices were moreover a constant source of embarrassment. Convinced that Chamberlain would back up his firm stand, the French compromised their design on the Niger basin and signed the Niger Convention in June 1898. The agreement virtually ended the scramble for West Africa. Now all that the imperialists had to do was occupy the territories drawn on the maps in London and Paris. This settlement came none too soon, for within three months the struggle to control the Nile came to a climax. The French had reached Fashoda.

FASHODA

In September 1895 Captain J. P. Marchand, with the support of the permanent officials of the Colonial Ministry, revived the Monteil Mission and proposed to lead a French expedition to the Upper Nile. The project met with a cool reception at first but was finally approved in the spring of 1896 following a change of government in France. Marchand left for Africa in June. The march to Fashoda had begun, but Marchand was not alone. King Leopold had never abandoned his Nile quest, and although his forces had retired from Wadelai in 1892, he laid plans in the summer of 1895 for a new assault. Led by Baron Dhanis, the Congo-Nile expedition was to march from Stanleyville to the Nile and then down the river to Fashoda. Unhappily, Dhanis attempted to pass through the terrifying rain forest of the Aruwimi valley. Here his troops mutinied, and although a second column under Captain Louis Chaltin eventually reached the Nile at Rejaf and drove off the Mahdist defenders, Chaltin had neither the men nor the supplies to push northward to Fashoda.

While the French and the Belgians made their way laboriously toward the Upper Nile, the British became increasingly alarmed by the threats to the Nile coming from both east and west. The defeat at Aduwa had ended the immediate threat to Ethiopia, but it opened the door to French influence. The French wanted the Nile; Menelik II wanted to expand his own domain. Together they presented yet another challenge to the security of the Nile and the British position in Egypt. With Marchand pressing up the Ubangi and Nile tributaries from the west and several French expeditions preparing to march from Ethiopia in the east, Lord Salisbury, who had returned to power in 1895, began to apply all his diplomatic skill and political acumen to defend the Nile. He had two options: to conquer the Mahdists in the Sudan at great expense and bloodshed or to send a flying column from East Africa down the Nile to Fashoda. Salisbury had always preferred to defend the Nile from East Africa rather than from Egypt, but when the construction of the Uganda Railway from Mombasa to Lake Victoria was delayed and Captain Macdonald's expedition from East Africa to the Nile was diverted in Uganda, the prime minister ordered General H. H. Kitchener and his Anglo-Egyptian army into the Sudan.

In 1896 Kitchener had conducted a limited, but successful, campaign along the Dongola Reach in the northern Sudan. Here he paused to consolidate his base, to construct the all-important railway across the Nubian Desert, and to strengthen his army with British battalions. By 1898 Kitchener was ready, and in February he received orders to advance. In April the Anglo-Egyptian forces defeated the Mahdists at the Atbara River and, after waiting through the heat of summer in the Sudan, pressed on to the Mahdist capital of Omdurman. On the plains of Karari outside the city the machine guns of Kitchener's army destroyed the massed host of the Khalifa Abd Allahi. With imperturbable courage the Mahdists charged the line of Anglo-Egyptian troops, and with matchless bravery they died. By noon on September 2, 1898, the Mahdist state was no more. Kitchener had come none too soon. Marchand had reached Fashoda.

Accompanied by a flotilla of gunboats and troop-laden steamers, Kitchener hurried up the Nile to confront Marchand. Their meeting was cordial, but the results were not. Fashoda was the most dangerous Anglo-French confrontation in nearly a century and the most serious crisis in Africa between European rivals. Britain was united and determined to secure the Nile. France was divided and hesitant to precipitate a European war over a mud-hut village on the edge of a swamp hundreds of miles from the nearest French possession. The French gave way, and after drawn out negotiations with King Leopold, which lasted until 1906, the Nile became safely British.

While this drama was being played out in the swamps of the Southern Sudan and in the chancelleries of Europe, an equally important and more bloody struggle was taking place in South Africa. An economic interpretation of European imperialism appears at first glance to be the most meaningful explanation for the British acquisition of central and southern Africa. The great profits that Rhodes derived from his diamond monopoly at Kimberley helped to finance his gold-mining operations in the Transvaal, to provide the capital for the acquisition of Rhodesia by his British South Africa Company, and to support British imperialism in Nyasaland and north of the Zambezi. The picture of Rhodes as the archetypal economic man, the prototype Hobsonian seizing new lands for investment, takes little account, however, of Rhodes' expansive vision of a British empire stretching from Cape Town to Cairo, an empire that would bring Anglo-Saxon civilization to darkest Africa as much as it would exploit black labor for white profits. His critics might dismiss such dreams as an imaginary by-product of bourgeois self-interest, but no one can deny the powerful influence of such dreams on Rhodes' quest for empire.

Indeed, Rhodes' imperialism was more failure than success. His haste to bring the independent Transvaal within the British empire precipitated the Jameson Raid, with disastrous results. In 1896 Leander Starr Jameson and his filibustering troopers, paid and equipped by the British South Africa Company, burst into the Transvaal to overthrow the Boer government of Paul Kruger. The raiders ignominiously failed and were captured, deepening the division between Briton and Boer in South Africa and stimulating anticolonial feelings in Britain and throughout the world. Moreover, the failure of the raid stripped Rhodesia of its police forces, and the Matabele and Mashona, who had been organizing to resist the rather callous white domination, used the opportunity to revolt, threatening settler paramountcy in Central Africa and discrediting the administration of the British South Africa Company in Europe. The failure of Rhodes to build an empire in South Africa by manipulation forced the British government into a direct confrontation with the Boer farmers of the Transvaal, not to protect the gold mines or the British capital invested in them, but to secure the Cape and its hinterland as a vital strategic link in the imperial chains stretching eastward to India and northward to Central Africa. British gold investors had nothing to fear from the Boers, who had no intention of destroying the mining industry. The Boers did, however, fear the loss of their political supremacy, and in the end political questions, not economic considerations, precipitated the Anglo-Boer war. Although militarily victorious over bitter and fierce resistance by the Boer farmers, British imperialism suffered a disastrous political defeat. Politically, the war brought only discredit to British imperialists and the cause of empire they espoused. Although the war ended in the consolidation of British empire in South Africa, British imperialism never again recovered its popularity, and the British public turned increasingly to domestic social problems. The tropical empire was left to the upper and middle classes of Englishmen to administer as cheaply and quietly as possible. The economic promise of empire had become tarnished by its political failure in South Africa.

The partition of Africa was virtually complete. Only a handful of states on the periphery of the African continent remained free of European control, and by the outbreak of World War I only two countries, Liberia and Ethiopia, maintained their independence. Liberia was not only in one of the least attractive regions of the African continent, but she successfully played the European powers and the United States against one another to maintain a remarkable degree of independence. Ethiopian integrity was preserved more gloriously by the impressive victory at Aduwa, checking European imperialism on the Ethiopian plateau and permitting Menelik to consolidate his rule and to extend his control to the south and west. Not only was Aduwa the first major defeat for whites in Africa that could not be reversed, but the Ethiopian victory made a deep impression on the intellectuals of the black diaspora and on educated black South Africans. The other states, Morocco and Libya, had slipped under French and Italian administration respectively. France acquired Morocco in 1912, but only after facing two crises precipitated by German designs to assert imperial power for the sake of prestige; the acquisition resulted in the loss of large portions of the French Congo to the German Cameroons. Italy found compensation for the loss of Ethiopia, but not for their loss of prestige, in a desultory war with Turkey, which resulted in the annexation of Tripoli and Benghazi. Neither the Franco-German dispute over Morocco nor the Italian-Turkish struggle for Libya possessed the drama or the danger of the Fashoda crisis; they were, in fact, the peripheral and rather sandy remains of the scramble for the tropical regions farther south.

OCCUPATION, RESISTANCE, AND PACIFICATION

Once the European powers had partitioned Africa, they had to occupy the land and establish administrations. The imposition of such control was, of course, inherent in European imperialism, a logical consequence of the division of the African continent by rival negotiators in the chancelleries of Europe, and rationalized by humanitarian, economic, religious, and strategic arguments. At first the Europeans encountered little African resistance and, in fact, could hardly have overcome determined opposition. Virtually everywhere the initial European intruders aroused curiosity, if not suspicion, but created little conflict. They were, after all, few in number, accompanied by a handful of troops and porters, and they resembled more the expeditions of the European explorers than the agents of a great European power. Unwilling and unable to impose their authority by force, these early officials were required to negotiate rather than to conquer. By peaceful persuasion, tact, and the judicious bestowal of gifts, the Europeans sought to commit the local authorities to a course of action, the consequences of which the Africans rarely understood. Frequently, the Africans welcomed the Europeans as allies against local rivals, not realizing that the alliance would ultimately result in subservience. With few exceptions the coastal polities were in disarray and the beginning of the European occupation of Africa proceeded with little bloodshed on either side and few confrontations between the representatives of rival European nations.

The peaceful occupation of Africa could not last. On the one hand, the Europeans were required to increase substantially the size of their expeditionary forces in order to invade the interior of Africa, where the competition with rival European forces increased proportionately with the distance from the coast. On the other, the African states of the interior were larger, better organized, and more determined to resist the European occupation than were their coastal counterparts. Collisions between European and African forces became more frequent and more bloody as the numerical superiority of the African armies was dissipated before the automatic weapons of the Europeans. The initial, violent confrontation, which usually resulted in the submission of the African leaders, was frequently followed by protracted skirmishes, local rebellions, and, occasionally, guerilla warfare. Once again the technical superiority and self-confidence of the Europeans proved decisive. In addition, by playing on local African animosities and tribal rivalries and by using African troops, who often formed the vanguard of the European armies, the Europeans were able to overcome the difficulties of terrain, climate, and logistics in order to crush African resistance. Only on rare occasions did African states seek mutual support against the advancing Europeans, and when this occurred the agreements usually took the form of nonaggression pacts, like that between the sultan of Sokoto and Rabih Zubayr in 1897 to resist British and French encroachment, respectively, rather than real combinations of military resources to stand against a common enemy. Prolonged, often brutal, and expensive, the period of pacification that followed the partition of Africa did not come to its melancholy conclusion until the outbreak of World War I. Courageous but futile, African resistance increased in intensity from the first and rather feeble reaction in the western and central Sudan, the Congo, and East Africa, to the major conflicts in Madagascar, Ethiopia, and the Nile Valley, culminating in the bitter struggle between Briton and Boer in South Africa.

After the victorious battles the task of establishing an administration proved the least difficult in those states that, paradoxically, had offered the most coordinated and organized resistance. Once defeated, the same political organization that had been employed to oppose the European advance was just as effectively utilized by the Europeans to maintain order. Where such organization did not exist, the Europeans could not easily impose control and were, consequently, faced with a host of localized rebellions against their rule. Thus, Ahmadu Sefu, the son of Al-Hajj Umar, might hold off the French in the western Sudan, and the more redoubtable Mandingo Muslim, Samori, might lead the people of the upper Niger and Volta basins against the French until 1898, but their defeat was followed by the rapid implementation of French control. Further south, however, the Ivory Coast had become a French colony as early as 1893, but another twenty years elapsed before the French succeeded in pacifying the diffuse polities and stateless societies of the colony. Further east in the central Sudan the French faced similar problems in attempting to exert authority over the nomadic Taureg peoples. South of Lake Chad, however, Rabih Zubayr, a freebooter from the Nile Valley, had carved out an empire in Bagirmi and eastern Bornu in the 1890s. By 1900 three French expeditions from the Senegal, North Africa, and the Congo met near Lake Chad and killed Rabih in battle at Kusseri. His defeat was followed by the widespread acceptance of French administration by war-weary people in Bagirmi, while the exhausted Kanuri were unable to resist British control in Bornu. Even in Madagascar the breakup of the Merina Kingdom in the 1880s facilitated French encroachment but prolonged Malagasy resistance. By undermining Hova authority the French were required to suppress rebellions first against the Hova and then against themselves. In 1895 General J. S. Gallieni arrived from his victorious campaigns in West Africa, but nearly a decade of bitter and brutal fighting elapsed before the French were able to impose French rule on the fragmented remains of the Merina Kingdom.

The French experience was not unique. In northern Nigeria the British had to conquer those Fulani emirates that could not be induced to surrender peacefully. Thus, in 1897 the forces of the Royal Niger Company, under the leadership of Sir George Goldie himself, defeated the army of the Fulani Emir of Nupe and occupied his capital before routing the Fulani troops that were defending Ilorin. After Goldie's Company constabulary was taken over by the British government and reorganized as the West African Frontier Force, Lugard ordered it forward into the heartland of the Fulani empire of Sokoto, storming Yola, the capital of Adamawa in 1901, capturing the great city of Kano in 1903, and defeating the massed armies of the sultan himself before the walls of Sokoto. Although resistance from Burmi continued until that town was assaulted and the sultan killed, the Fulani pacifically accepted British overrule, while Lugard, in turn, largely preserved the Fulani political structure and employed Fulani institutions to achieve order and control.

A similar process took place after the conquest of Ashanti in 1896. The defeat of the Mahdist state in the Sudan in 1898 was followed by the British employment of tribal authorities for administration. But for another generation punitive expeditions proved necessary to pacify the Nilotic peoples of the Southern Sudan, whose stateless societies the British failed to understand. Having no comprehension of Nilotic society, British officials could not employ Nilotic institutions to assert control without continual recourse to military force. In East Africa the British, after victorious displays of military power, were able to utilize the political institutions of the sultan of Zanzibar and the interlacustrine kingdoms to affirm their authority in those regions. True, the implacable Kabarega, the Mukama, or ruler, of Bunyoro, resisted until 1899, but thereafter British control in Bunyoro remained unquestioned. British efforts to establish order and authority among the Nilotic-speaking, stateless societies of East Africa were less successful. A decade of punitive expeditions was required to pacify the Nandi. The Masai, decimated by disease and civil war, continued uncooperative, but quiescent; but the Suk, Karamojong, and Turkana repeatedly defied British authority for another generation.

The Germans were no more successful among East African peoples of diffuse political structures than were the British. No effective African political institutions or organizations existed with which to administer the coast after the suppression of a rebellion by Swahili-speaking Africans and Arabs in 1888 and 1889. In the interior the dearth of centralized African political units produced no indigenous political authorities to act as a buffer between German economic exploitation and the African peasants. Without political leadership African resistance was organized by the traditional spirit mediums of a cult system; these mediums brought together the diverse groups in the great Maji-Maji rebellion of 1905–1907, which seriously threatened German rule. In South-West Africa the Herero sustained an even more unified and heroic resistance to German imperial rule until nearly exterminated by German military forces in 1904.

Although the occupation of Central Africa was undertaken by Cecil Rhodes and his British South African Company, the establishment of European control followed a pattern similar to that between the imperial British government and African states in other regions of the African continent. The erosion of African authority began with a negotiated treaty between Rhodes' agents and Lobengula, the powerful chief of the Matabele, who controlled part of the plateau country between the Zambezi and the Limpopo rivers. In the treaty the European emissaries extracted concessions permitting Europeans to enter Mashonaland, a tributary region of the Matabele. Upon arriving in Mashonaland in 1890, the farming and mining settlers soon clashed with the Matabele, defeating them in 1893. Although both the Matabele and the Mashona appeared to have resigned themselves to the arrival of the Europeans, they were not prepared to accept the loss of land, cattle, pride, and political power. With their traditions of resistance and charismatic leadership and their past history of political centralization, the Matabele and Mashona revolted between 1886 and 1897. Led by the spirit mediums, who played a distinctive organizational role, the revolt proved the greatest challenge to European domination in eastern and southern Africa. Although the Matabele were defeated, they were not crushed, and in negotiations with Rhodes himself, the traditional leaders regained some of their authority, which was subsequently utilized by the British South Africa Company in administering the territory.

The effectiveness of alien rule over a conquered people is determined less by racial differences than by the similarities between the political institutions of ruler and ruled. Thus, in South Africa the imposition of British imperial rule upon the Boers of the Transvaal resulted in fierce resistance and guerilla warfare. Upon the defeat of the Boers in 1902, however, the structure and similarity between Boer political institutions and those of the British not only facilitated the establishment of imperial administration, but contributed to their self-government long before autonomy was ever considered for African territories farther north.

Thus, by the outbreak of World War I the European powers had not only partitioned the African continent but, with few exceptions, had successfully pacified it as well. Clearly, the partition had been made possible by the many long years of European contact on the coast, the exploration of the interior during the first three-quarters of the nineteenth century and, finally, the utilization of the new technology by merchants, missionaries, and soldiers during their advance into the hinterland. Thereafter, the partition was precipitated by a host of factors in Europe and Africa—political, economic, and personal—the emphasis of which varied from one region to another; no single explanation will suffice to explain events even in one region much less the entire continent.

Thus, while Britain's occupation of the Nile Valley and East Africa in the face of competition from Italy, Germany, France, and King Leopold's Congo Free State was governed primarily by the continuity of British strategic requirements to protect her life line to the East and her Oriental Empire, the occupation of eastern Africa was conditioned as well by the necessities of placating the imperialist business interests who sought long-range gain, glory, and security. In West Africa the strategic considerations were more subordinated to economic goals than in East Africa, but even on the coast where trade dominated African and European relationships, prestige and humanitarian concerns did much to shape events. National pride and individual glory played an even greater role than economic interests in the Western Sudan and in the Congo basin. Although the commercial schemes and subsequent exploitation of King Leopold conditioned the history of the Congo Free State, the scramble was dictated as much by Leopold's megalomania and French patriotic enthusiasm as by the profits derived from the collection of rubber. In South and Central Africa as well, Cecil Rhodes and later Joseph Chamberlain and Lord Milner were not solely motivated by economic considerations. Questions of security, strategy, and the political vision of a unified southern Africa attracted and shaped the decisions of these imperialists as much as profits.

Pacification was the inexorable corollary to partition and resulted directly from it. The success of pacification depended as much on the nature of African institutions as on European technological superiority, and its effectiveness relied as much on the utilization of African political structures as on European administration. The European rulers had to have African cooperation or, at least, acquiescence; to obtain it, they had to fight resistance and to compromise with both collaborators and resistors. Thus, the partition, which had largely taken place in Europe, and pacification, which by necessity was shaped by both European and African activities, have deeply conditioned the subsequent periods of colonial rule and independence. For better or worse, the peoples of both continents were suddenly exposed to new ideas and institutions that challenged their traditional ways of life. The Europeans were in control of Africa.

Chapter 4

European
Rule

The conquest of Africa was carried out by African and European troops under the command of white officers. Invested with both civil and military powers, these officers were responsible for establishing the beginnings of European administration as African resistance diminished into sullen acquiescence. In these early days, courage, independence, and endurance were more important qualifications for ruling than imagination, understanding, and efficiency. Order was the primary requirement, and the peace was frequently maintained as much by the strength of character and personality of the individual officers as by force of arms. If the Africans sought to challenge the imperial authorities openly, then armed punitive patrols were employed, which civilian officials were ill-equipped by training and temperament to lead. The administrative units of colonial Africa were immense, communications were hazardous, and the colonial state machineries were so fragile that the attitudes and personalities of the individual officials played a central role in determining the character of the administration.

THE RULERS The European officer enjoyed considerable freedom to rule his district in splendid isolation, unless its tranquility was disturbed by an outbreak of disorder that required troops from the provincial headquarters or administrative interference from the capital. Under such conditions these officials assumed, sometimes unconsciously, the role of paternal autocrat and benevolent despot. They hammered out peace, fought off innumerable diseases, and paid little heed to the egregious administrative orders from the central government. Their way of life attracted the self-sufficient individual—the officer who could shoot, but who did not need the companionship of the mess; the man who was resilient to loneliness, yet capable of the sympathy needed to win the obedience of the people, his subjects. In these isolated circumstances some European officials succumbed to drink or drugs. Others took advantage of their position to abuse the villagers and their women. The overwhelming majority, however, adjusted to conditions, asserted their authority, and earned at least the acquiescence and often the loyalty and respect of the Africans.

Although military officers continued to serve in the colonial administrations, their numbers and influence steadily diminished as civilians were recruited to staff the increasing bureaucracy of the African colonies. In British Africa civilian officials were sought mainly from the British universities, particularly from Oxford and Cambridge, and from the public schools, but those who went out to Africa were characterized not so much by their intellectual brilliance as by their qualities of leadership and physical stamina. To be sure, sound, competent, steady men were clearly desirable for service in the remote regions of Africa, but the accumulation of men of similar intellectual achievement tended to encourage conformity rather than creativity, duty rather than initiative, paternalism rather than tutelage. Moreover, the social class and family origins of these British officials were nearly as uniform as their education, abilities, and attitudes. They came mostly from county families, from members of the imperial civil service, or from professional classes whose origins and traditions were in the English countryside. They considered themselves "gentlemen," and whatever the social origins of their families, they assumed the duties, responsibilities, and social prerogatives of gentlemen. The devotion to duty, the love of the out of doors, the responsibility to care for the village poor, and even the enthusiasm for village cricket shaped the assumptions and created the confidence to rule, which were later sustained and confirmed by education at public school and the university. Infused from birth with the responsibility to serve and to rule, whether in an English country hamlet or an African village, the concepts of paternalism and trusteeship were as natural as they were unconscious parts of life.

Having accepted benevolent stewardship as the proper relationship between men in a society in which a few were destined by birth and training to rule, British officials were, not surprisingly, conservative in thought and manner. However, they did not resist change either in Britain or in Africa, although change was preferred to be selective and evolutionary. The slow, gradual transformation of society within the context of one's traditional way of life was to a British official both proper and sensible. All his experience and traditions confirmed the wisdom of development along the lines of Tory conservatism rather than radical democracy. His education at Oxford or Cambridge served to cement these ideas and encase them with an enormous confidence in their efficacy, a confidence without which so few could never have ruled so many. Certainly administrators of such backgrounds and educations could hardly be expected to initiate or to adopt radical programs. No trustee could be a radical by policy when he was a conservative by instinct and belief. Indeed, the few bold and imaginative schemes of social and economic change during the early years of British rule—the Gezira cotton-growing scheme in the Sudan, educational development on the Gold Coast—ironically were initiated by military engineers, Sir H. H. Kitchener in the Sudan and Sir Gordon Guggisberg in the Gold Coast.

The lack of understanding and even hostility between civilian British officials and the new class of educated Africans should not be surprising. Clearly, the Africans for which British officials had the closest affinity were the traditional rulers of African society. Thrown together in the early years of administration, the British officials found close and enduring friendships among those tribal authorities whose political and social beliefs, not to mention personalities and character, were, in spite of the cultural differences, strikingly similar to their own. Convinced that gradual, evolutionary development was the only sure road to progress, the British official could hardly be expected to do more than tolerate the new African elite, divorced from their traditional society and educated in the politics of radical democracy and the economics of socialism.

French administrators in Africa were men of very different educational and social backgrounds from their British counterparts. They were essentially lower-middle class in origin, poorly educated, and frequently in compromised positions or incapable of making a living in France. Unlike service in the British empire, the French colonial service had little prestige or tradition and never attracted the French aristocracy, which was vociferously opposed to the overseas expansion of the Third Republic. The recruitment of officials was haphazard and depended a great deal on political patronage. Before 1900 only a third of the officials had completed a secondary education, and by 1914 only about half. Even the establishment of an African training program at the Ecole Coloniale, which had been founded in 1892 to train administrators for Indochina, did not resolve the educational deficiencies, since not all administrators for Africa were selected from candidates who were graduates of the school.

The attitudes of these middle-class French functionaries were of even greater importance in the administration of France's African empire than was their education or lack of it. Imbued with the traditions of the gentry, British officials possessed empathy, if not respect, for the chiefs, whereas the lower-middle-class attitudes of the French officials manifested a bourgeois contempt for the traditional African authorities, whom they regarded as feudal anachronisms or monarchial despots. Most French administrators were suspicious of chiefs, doubtful of their loyalty to France, and aroused by their "exploitation" of their own people.

Although both British and French officials were authoritarian in practice, the source of European paternalism, which was later transformed in vague notions of trusteeship, differed dramatically between each nation's administrators. The nostalgic sympathy of the British for African rulers and their general respect for African customs, language, and authority was contrasted by the French belief in the superiority of French culture and in the egalitarian traditions of the Republican middle class, which underlay French distrust of the chiefs and disdain for things African. For the French, the logical alternative to trusteeship was to impose French language and culture upon African societies. Although such action was revolutionary in design, it proved intensely conservative in character. Although the chief was relegated to a secondary role in the administration—contemptuously dismissed as a subordinate official in a highly centralized empire —this hierarchical structure was not employed to change as much as to conserve. This was perhaps best reflected in the conservatism of the members of the colonial service in the interwar period, during which the innovative and bold spirit of the nineteenth-century imperialists was lost.

Although better educated, the young men who came to Africa from France after World War I served an apprenticeship under older, more experienced officers stationed in the bush. The older officers deeply inculcated junior officers with the doctrines they had followed, and, for the most part, the younger men continued to rule according to these doctrines, despite the rapidly changing conditions in the French colonies. Moreover, when European wives came and paperwork increased dramatically, French administrators tended to be isolated from the Africans and the relationships between them were solidified. This rigidity not only made the French administrations conservative, but also perpetuated the deep belief in the moral superiority of French culture, which was translated by the enlightened few into a vague idea of trusteeship, but which demonstrated to the many the justification for continuing French control.

Belgian and German administrators possessed many of the assumptions of their French and British counterparts but differed in the attitude with which they exerted their authority. Both in the Congo and in the German colonies officials were drawn largely from the Belgian and German armies. For a time King Leopold also employed Italian officers. Most of the officials had been noncommissioned officers and, not surprisingly, had transmitted to Africa the attitudes of the parade ground and the standards of the barracks. They believed in the use of force and were contemptuous of African culture, which was measured more by the ineffectiveness of African weapons than by its social and artistic complexities. Many of the German officers were Prussians, who regarded the Africans with the disdain traditionally reserved for Slavic peasants. Although the higher Belgian administrators were usually of French extraction, the lower echelons were staffed largely with Flemings, who tended to adopt the attitudes and the means of administration more akin to their Teutonic neighbors than to those from France.

After World War II there was a perceptible change in the men who came out from Europe to rule Africa. Ostensibly, they came from the same class, with similar, if not more, education than their predecessors, but in reality they were not the same. Reared in an age of worldwide economic depression and devastating world war, and educated in schools and universities where radical ideas competed with the traditional curriculum, they viewed the world differently from their seniors. Gone were the confidence and faith in the imperial mission that had sustained so many of the early officials during difficult and lonely times. World War II had irreparably damaged the firm belief in the superiority of European administration and the wisdom of European paternal rule, and many of the new men who came to Africa were inclined to think that perhaps the Africans could manage just as well without European officials to supervise them. Able to foresee independence for Africa, these men more readily came to terms with the intellectual elite from whom the future rulers of Africa were clearly to come, but they were too few in number and too junior in status to have much influence on the great decision that led to self-government, self-determination, and independence. It is perhaps just as well, for although these men could more easily adapt to the changing circumstances in Africa, they probably did not possess sufficient confidence to carry on European imperial rule, even if the Africans had consented. To them, trusteeship was a political principle, not a way of life.

THE DUAL MANDATE   Although the cultural differences between French and British officials produced dramatically different approaches to the day-to-day administration of the colonies, the principles of trusteeship did not depend only on British paternalism or French moral superiority. The idea of responsible empire was as old as European overseas expansion itself, and it went far deeper than sentimental appeals to the "white man's burden" and the "civilizing mission." Although the motives for responsibility and accountability in empire ranged from guilt to ethnocentric pride, nebulous notions of trusteeship emerged at the end of World War I in the political reality of the mandate system established under the League of Nations to administer the conquered German and Turkish colonies and dependencies. To some, the mandate system was little more than an artful device to perpetuate European imperialism. To others, the mandates represented the practical realization of the idea of trusteeship, since the mandatory power was responsible to a constituted authority, the Permanent Mandates Commission of the League of Nations. To be sure, neither the League nor the Mandates Commission ever possessed the necessary authority to impose international control on the mandatory powers in Africa, but the idea of trust had been translated into a reality, however tenuous, which could no longer be ignored by colonial thinkers and practitioners. Henceforth, in policy and practice, ethical considerations conditioned European administration and helped to check excesses of European national interests in Africa.

The most influential expression of imperial responsibility was Lord Lugard's *The Dual Mandate in British Tropical Africa*, which became the manual and inspiration for British administration in Africa during the interwar years. To Lugard, the first responsibility of the advanced nations, and particularly of Great Britain, was to impart the moral and ethical foundations of civilized nations to backward peoples. The second obligation was to pursue the material development of technologically primitive peoples. Lugard's combination of economic development and ethical principles was not confined solely to the British empire. In France Albert Sarraut's influential *La Mise en valeur des colonies française* emphasized the benefits of the development of backward territories not only for France, but for the world. Although the moral superiority of European nations was regarded as the only legitimate basis for sovereignty over more primitive peoples, this moral superiority embodied the responsibility for tutelage and the accountability for just administration. Despite its self-evident paternalism and the dearth of any declared goal of self-government, which trusteeship clearly implied, the Dual Mandate represented the new attitude toward colonialism of those European officials who came to Africa during the interwar years. Less confident than their Victorian predecessors in their ability to rule and more aware and appreciative of other cultures due to the work of anthropologists, these colonial officials were, at the same time, subjected to increasing criticism from socialists in Britain and France who insisted upon colonial reforms and even cast doubt on the value or purpose of imperialism. The immediate impact of these ideas, assumptions, and criticisms produced an enthusiasm for colonial administration that soon transformed widely applied colonial practice into a doctrinaire colonial theory known as "indirect rule."

INDIRECT
RULE

In brief, indirect rule was the practice by which an imperial power administered a foreign population by ruling through the traditional leaders and preserving and utilizing the indigenous institutions. The technique was as old as empire itself and was employed by the British in India and the Orient long before it was applied to Africa. In Africa it was first introduced systematically into Northern Nigeria by Lord Lugard as an obvious solution to practical problems. Lugard had few administrators and little money to govern a vast and populous land. To impose a British bureaucracy in order to implement alien laws and justice was as politically impractical as it was financially impossible. Lugard, therefore, retained the existing political and social system by which the Fulani emirs had ruled their Hausa subjects. The British controlled the emirs through inconspicuously influential British political officers who were resident at court and who governed by working with and through the traditional authorities. Governing indirectly proved not only cheap, but effective. British rule was secured; the country was peaceful and orderly.

The dramatic success of indirect rule in Northern Nigeria resulted in its widespread application throughout British Africa. Indirect rule transformed what had been a practical expedient to maintain control in Nigeria into the well-developed theory for governing alien peoples that Lugard popularized in *The Dual Mandate*. After World War I indirect rule was systematically applied to eastern Nigeria, Sierra Leone, Northern Rhodesia, Nyasaland, the Gold Coast, Tanganyika, Uganda, and the Southern Sudan, where it "passed through three stages, first of a useful administrative device, than that of a political doctrine, and finally that of a religious dogma." * During the 1920s

---

* Lord Hailey, "Some Problems Dealt with in *An African Survey*," in *International Affairs* (March/April, 1939), p. 202.

British colonial officials came to accept uncritically the principles of indirect rule, while their superiors in the Colonial Office defended them with unswerving confidence. By the 1930s indirect rule had become the panacea for all the problems of governing a vast African empire. Its advocates were not without cause for their faith in indirect rule.

Despite its pragmatic origins, indirect rule embodied considerable theoretical advantages. First, it recognized the abilities of conquered peoples at a time when anthropology had made European appreciation of other cultures not only popular, but respectable. Second, indirect rule accepted and employed indigenous institutions within the larger structure of imperial administration. European officials guided, supervised, and encouraged the evolution of these institutions to meet changing conditions that might otherwise have destroyed those institutions. Indirect rule was never meant simply to preserve the status quo, but rather to permit the progressive evolution of African society while maintaining a balance between continuity and change. Its principles had wide support from Europeans who had divergent social and political opinions. Conservative administrators who feared an alienated elite educated only to make trouble expected the indigenous authorities to make the empire safe for autocracy. Anthropologists who proclaimed the value of traditional institutions naturally approved of their preservation. European liberals who were vociferous opponents of imperialism saw the ideals of trusteeship and the implications of self-government in the doctrines of indirect rule. Even the missionaries looked to indirect rule as a shield against the corrupting influences produced by modernization and social change.

The practice of indirect rule was not confined solely to British Africa. Both the Belgians and the French governed indirectly, but not as enthusiastically as their British counterparts. Although intensely empirical and inclined to be hierarchical and bureaucratic, Belgian administration in the Congo recognized indigenous authority in principle, and the traditional leaders were regarded as the link between the Africans and the Belgian officials. As in Northern Nigeria the very size of the Congo and the paucity of trained European officials precluded any other alternative, and in 1910 the colony was divided into *chefferies* under a chief, who in turn was subject to European supervision. Although the selected chief frequently had little traditional claim to the position and soon became more a petty official of the government than the leader of his people, Belgian officials continued until late in the interwar period to assert that the progressive evolution of the African could only take place within his own culture and institutions. This same policy, of course, permitted the Belgians to rule an immense colony with few men and comparatively little expense.

Although the principles of indirect rule were widely advocated and applied during the interwar years, the practice came under increasing criticism. Irreconcilable contradictions existed between the theory of indirect rule as conceived by senior officials in Africa and Europe and its application by the officers in the local administrative districts. In those areas where a hierarchical political structure had existed in precolonial Africa, as in Northern Nigeria, indirect rule functioned effectively. In many regions of Africa, however, political units were small, and traditional authority was diffuse and restricted. Among stateless societies, chiefs were unknown. Thus, either to conform to the principles of indirect rule or to establish European authority at the local level, as in the case of the Belgian Congo, "chiefs" were appointed and imposed upon peoples to whom the institution was unknown and unwanted. In these instances indirect rule was reduced to an administrative convenience in which the mechanics of administration proved more important than the preservation of indigenous political institutions and social customs, which were often destroyed rather than preserved or encouraged to evolve. Frequently, indirect rule produced stagnation in African society rather than the progressive development envisaged by its proponents. Confirmed and even invested with greater powers by the European rulers, the traditional authorities became the upholders of the status quo at a time when social mobility and new educational opportunities were creating an educational elite outside the traditional society and alienated from it. With those positions open to Africans in the native administration that was monopolized by the traditional authorities, there was no room for the younger, better-educated Africans who were more prepared to adapt to social change than were the hereditary leaders. Finally, indirect rule simply could not work in the new towns that sprang up all over Africa around the centers of European administration. In these urban locations the British and the Belgians were as assimilationist as the French, and municipal government was established on European models.

Despite these deficiencies, indirect rule must be judged by what it prevented as much as by what it failed to accomplish. Inherent in its principles were the ideas of cooperation and trusteeship, which helped check brutality, arbitrary injustice, and imperious intervention. Indirect rule was a genuine attempt at the devolution of power, without which more repugnant and abusive social and economic exploitation could have been carried out in the name of civilization. To be sure, the colonial ruler possessed the ultimate authority, but his power was not absolute. Indirect rule not only made the distribution of that power possible, minimizing the opportunities for corruption inherent in absolute power, but also mitigated against the corrosive effects of authority exercised directly from the center.

ASSIMILATION AND ASSOCIATION

Torn between past policy and present reality, French administrative policy remained clear in principle and confused in practice. Springing from the democratic egalitarianism of the Revolution, French colonial thinking in the nineteenth century had been dominated by the policy of assimilation by which Africans were to become French-speaking citizens inhabiting territories directly controlled from Paris and embracing one large and indivisible republic. Moreover, unlike the British who had a firm belief in the importance of local government, the French have traditionally regarded local autonomy as a centrifugal force that threatened the unity of the nation. Culturally, assimilation was quite impossible except for a few individual Africans, and France could never have Gallified the masses. Politically and economically, assimilation was less of a foregone failure. French administration of her African territories was characterized by uniform, centralized rule from Paris, and close economic ties were forged by common tariffs and an active intervention in the local economies. Despite the coherence and symmetry of French colonial policy, there existed wide variations on the local level and among the attitudes and actions of French officials.

Even before World War I the ideal of assimilation was giving way to the reality of African diversity. Many French officials argued cogently that colonial policy should vary according to local needs and should be characterized by cooperation rather than coercion. General Joseph S. Gallieni advocated using indigenous authorities in Madagascar, and his protégé, General Louis Lyautey, employed traditional leaders in Morocco. Both administrations were extraordinarily successful, providing concrete examples for the critics of assimilation, and resulting in a significant shift to a French version of indirect rule, officially defined as a policy of association.

Politically, "association" meant that the indigenous authorities would exercise power, while the European officials would remain aloof, interceding only to check any abuse of that power. Economically, association was to be a collaboration between Frenchmen and Africans, the former providing the organization and technological skill, the latter giving their labor. Culturally, association never overcame its ambiguities. The work of Lucien Lévy-Bruhl, Maurice Delafosse, and the scholars of the French Institute of Black Africa (Institut français d'Afrique Noire, IFAN) clearly stimulated an interest and appreciation of African cultures, which, however, never replaced the firm belief in the superiority of the French language and culture. Although association resembled indirect rule in theory and French colonial thinkers extolled its principles in terms that British proponents of indirect rule would have approved, French administration in practice remained directed from the top down through a pyramidal bureaucracy to the lowest level—the chiefs, who continued to be more the agents of French administration than the leaders of their people. At the level where the ruling power meets the people, the imperial administration met its true test: Here the French political officer continued to intervene more directly in the affairs of the people than did his British counterpart. The language of administration and instruction was French, not the African vernacular. The French stressed the uniformity of their administration and its centralized control. The British, on the contrary, prided themselves in the diversity and devolutionary character of their African administrations.

DIRECT RULE   Whereas the British, French, and Belgians ruled indirectly in varying degrees and officially acknowledged the existence of indigenous authorities north of the Zambezi, European administration in Southern Rhodesia and South Africa was direct in theory and in practice and reflected the attitudes and assumptions of the European settlers. The settlers regarded African customs and institutions with repugnance, thinking them not only backward, but dangerous to European control. Even the colonial officials in Southern Rhodesia were not as inclined to utilize African institutions in the task of administration as were their counterparts in the British Colonial Office. To them, Africans were to be liberated from the restrictions of custom and freed from the tyranny of barbarous institutions. Not surprisingly, disinclination to preserve African practices ran counter to the trend toward indirect rule in the other African territories and clashed violently with the views of anthropologists, missionaries, and philanthropists who sought to preserve indigenous cultures. Equipped with a considerable degree of self-government that had been granted by the British government upon the abolition of administration by the British South African Company in 1923, direct rule in Southern Rhodesia radiated from Salisbury, its capital, not London, and was characterized by efficiency and paternalism, though it was not always unsympathetic nor oppressive. Nevertheless, by 1923 the alienation of nearly a third of the land to European settlers not only forced the Africans into less fertile areas, but had a deleterious impact on their customary institutions.

EXPLOITATION
OR
DEVELOPMENT?

If the first duty of the European rulers was to establish a moral order as the foundation of civilization, the second obligation imposed upon them by the Dual Mandate was to improve the material well-being of their African subjects. Most European administrators believed that modernization in the African colonies could only be carried out by direct aid from the state. To combat disease and illiteracy, to develop raw materials and industry, and to introduce scientific farming, large amounts of capital were required in all the colonies, which private enterprise could neither provide nor raise from other sources. Unfortunately, the nineteenth-century empire was predicated on the assumption that each colony must pay its own way and at no time be a burden upon the home country or its taxpayers. Since the indigenous African economies were characteristically subsistence level, little capital was available for investment in their own development. Unable to depend either upon internal savings or external grants in aid, the colonial administrations in Africa were forced to borrow development capital. Bond issues guaranteed by the home governments were consequently floated on the European money markets with considerable success, but, regrettably, the sums raised in this manner were limited and irregular, designed more to finance specific projects than long-range development plans.

Private investment, of course, was not excluded, but except for railroads and mining in south-central Africa, there were few resources in Africa to attract private capital. Despite the high rates of interest earned by venture capital on the African continent, Africa was not the El Dorado that the nineteenth-century advocates of empire had made it out to be, and European investors could easily find more profitable and more secure opportunities elsewhere. Before the outbreak of World War II, foreign investment in Africa totaled only $6 billion, most of which flowed into Africa during the interwar decades despite the worldwide economic depression of the 1930s. Therefore, although these years were not completely economically stagnant, foreign investment in Africa comprised only an insignificant percentage of total European overseas investment, limited to a few countries, and concentrated largely in mines and railroads.

Whether financed privately or by the state, railroads in Africa generated considerable enthusiasm among European investors by combining the romantic vision of binding together a wild continent by steel rails with the gleaming promise of profits derived from the transportation of manufactured goods and raw materials in and out of Africa. Colonial officials were more practical. To them, railroads were not only iron bands to unify disparate territories delimited by artificial frontiers and possessing little internal homogeneity for economic development, but also the means to move troops rapidly through the colony when needed to subdue the population and to keep order. Before the outbreak of World War II over 32,000 miles of track had been laid, but like foreign investment in general, two-thirds of the mileage was limited to southern Africa, where it served the mining industry.

Not surprisingly, nearly half (42 percent) of the funds invested in Africa before World War II were concentrated in South Africa. By the end of the nineteenth century the discovery and development of diamond- and gold-mining industries had created in South Africa the infrastructure—transportation, ports, effective systems of commercial exchange and finance—necessary for rapid economic development in the twentieth century. More important, South Africa possessed not only rich mineral resources, particularly gold, but also a large number of skilled workers who had emigrated from Europe and an even larger pool of cheap African labor. In the ten years between 1926 and 1936 South Africa nearly doubled the value of its gold production, providing the investors with profits and the government with enormous revenues for development. Not only did the South African economy expand at a time when manufacturing in other nations had shrunk during the Depression, but this expansion produced a dramatic increase in the number of secondary industries throughout the country.

If South Africa attracted and generated capital with gold, Northern Rhodesia and the Congo accomplished the same with copper. Although the first decade of copper mining in Northern Rhodesia brought no returns in the 1920s and little during the early 1930s, the end of the Depression and the economic boom created by World War II brought handsome profits to long-suffering investors. In the Congo copper production developed in the Katanga Province during the first decade of the twentieth century and particularly after the railroad from the Portuguese port of Beira reached Elizabethville. The increased demand for copper during World War I was followed by a mild slump and then the Great Depression from which the industry did not fully recover until World War II. Thereafter, the Copper Belt produced profits and prosperity, a portion—albeit a small portion—of which provided housing, schools, and medical facilities for the growing class of African skilled and semiskilled industrial workers.

Railroads and mining transformed the economy of southern and central Africa. The enterprises were organized by large foreign-owned corporations that could mobilize the vast amounts of capital and human skills required to provide the facilities and to train the Africans. The companies built houses, hospitals, and schools that neither the early colonial regimes nor smaller concerns could afford. The very size of these combines enabled them to plan, produce, and market ore and to overcome fluctuations in demand. Clearly, large-scale mining created wealth that the traditional means of production in a subsistence economy could never have accomplished. Ore that cannot be extracted from the earth has no value, and by mining gold, copper, and other metals, the Europeans were, in fact, not only changing, but developing the economy, providing compensatory advantages in return for profitable assets. The question is not so much whether the extractive industries "exploited" the dependency of African societies, but whether the advantages gained by those societies outweighed the assets, both human and material, that were lost. The charge of exploitation is more a matter of practices than of ideological principles, and the criticism of large-scale mining in Africa must necessarily concern the means of European enterprise rather than the ends.

European settlers in the past, African leaders in the present, the socialists at all times have accused the big mining companies of amassing huge profits by exploiting African labor. Labor, of course, was cheap because it was plentiful and unskilled, but low wages were not so much the result of artificially depressed wage scales as they were the result of a subsistence economy. So long as the African possessed the freedom to choose to work, he was subject to the law of supply and demand. Collectivization and compulsory labor would not necessarily have increased real wages and most certainly would have eliminated choice. In fact, during the early years of European rule in Africa many colonial governments employed forced labor in which wages and productivity were low. When the use of compulsory labor was gradually abandoned after World War I, the increasing supervision imposed by the imperial authorities on contracts and conditions of work tended to increase wages. Certainly, Africans could have been more ruthlessly used by European companies had they not been policed by imperial administrators who were sensitive to humanitarian critics at home. The failure to have any such check on the administration and the commercial companies in King Leopold's Congo Free State led to the most brutal treatment of Africans in the collection of rubber. In the extractive industries there is no doubt that the wages for black Africans were retarded by the restrictive practices of white workers who kept Africans out of certain branches of skilled employment, but such limitations were more the work of socialist trade unions than capitalist mine owners. Nevertheless, most critics have agreed that such means of exploitation can only end when the state plans, develops, produces, and markets African products for the benefit of the Africans and not just for the profits of a few alien financiers.

Given the fact that metropolitan governments before World War II were not prepared to provide capital for economic development, their African territories would have remained economically stagnant if European investment had been discouraged or restricted. Merely perpetuating the subsistence economy would have made the material improvement envisaged by the Dual Mandate a hollow mockery. The price of European capital was usually higher interest rates than those asked for enterprise in Europe, but the colonies were never forced to pay outrageous rates of interest. Indeed, their colonial status provided an element of financial security and, consequently, more favorable rates than independent states in Asia, Africa, and Latin America. To be sure, the difference between the rate of interest the African colonies had to pay and what was paid in Europe can be regarded as "exploitative," but it was a necessary requirement if risk capital was to rush in where metropolitan governments and cautious private investors feared to tread. Clearly, Britain did not need her African colonies in order to survive as a trading nation, as some mid-Victorians had argued in the nineteenth century and many Marxists assert today. Until the 1930s the British empire rested upon free trade, and no system of monopoly existed that would have made possible artificially contrived high profits for metropolitan merchants. In fact, consumers and producers bought and sold wherever they received the most favorable terms. No special favors were granted to British capitalists, and investment was generally welcomed from any source. Ironically, the very principles of free trade that prevented the British colonies from becoming mercantile monopolies have been criticized for stifling indigenous industrialization by not permitting the colonies to protect their own infant industries and traditional crafts against cheap European exports. Such disadvantages of free trade were not, however, the specific result of British imperialism, for totally independent states were forced to reduce tariff duties to the benefit of European manufactured goods. These disadvantages to free trade reflected the simple preponderance of European influence throughout the non-Western world rather than the iniquities of formal empire. Moreover, the inhabitants of European dependencies in tropical Africa possessed neither the technological skills nor the capital to embark upon an industrial revolution. These basic ingredients for modernization had to be brought to Africa from Europe before the European rulers or their African successors could begin to transform the subsistence economies of Africa.

AGRICULTURE   Although socialist critics of imperial rule in Africa have argued that state planning and industrial development are fundamental requirements for prosperity, the agricultural schemes of African peasants, European settlers, and large-scale plantation companies have demonstrated that a real increase in the standard of living need not necessarily be dependent upon industrialization. Before and after World War I there was an impressive increase in African agricultural exports. The most dramatic rise appeared on the Gold Coast after World War I and in South Africa after World War II, but throughout the African continent agricultural growth remained steady despite enormous environmental obstacles. Many regions of Africa suffered alternative cycles of downpour and drought, and all areas experienced a host of animal, plant, and human diseases; their disabilities were further compounded by the lack of rail and riverine transport. Despite the contributions of European settlers to the development of agriculture in Africa, the African peasant farmer proved to be more diversified in agricultural techniques and production. The variety of crops discouraged specialization in crop production and marketing organization so that the overwhelming majority of African farmers continued to cultivate the soil to exhaustion, confident that nature would restore fertility or that the abundance of land would enable them to move on to fallow fields. Neither procedure was conducive to the growth of a cash crop for the acquisition of capital.

In a few regions of Africa, however, agricultural specialization was not only accepted, but resulted in cash crops that produced the capital for the economic growth of the colonies. The development of cocoa in the Gold Coast and peanuts in Senegal by African peasant farmers required foresight, planning, and business acumen—precisely those qualities that past detractors have frequently insisted black Africans do not possess. The cacao tree was first carried from South America to São Tomé and Fernando Po by the Portuguese and then brought to the Guinea coast in 1879, where the plant flourished in the hot, humid climate. At the outbreak of World War II the Gold Coast colony was exporting half the world's cocoa supply. The prosperity derived from the cocoa trade enabled the colony to purchase materials and machinery previously unknown to the African inhabitants and without which modernization would have been impossible.

Peanuts were for Senegal what cocoa was for the Gold Coast. They were introduced in Senegal from Central America around 1820, and their cultivation was undertaken by African peasant farmers. Responding to the increasing demand of the French soap manufacturers for peanut oil, Africans produced nearly 5,000,000 kilograms by mid-century. The French administration encouraged peanut cultivation by developing superior seeds, introducing new agricultural techniques, and providing marketing and educational facilities through government-organized cooperative societies. Although the industry suffered during the Depression, Senegal became one of the world's great peanut producers, laying the foundations for future modernization. Despite the increasing dependence of African farmers upon guaranteed prices and markets, upon a single cash crop to the neglect of the traditional food-producing plants, and upon migrant labor that consumed potential profits, African agricultural enterprise in West Africa developed and prospered and for the first time in history participated and became a significant factor in the world economy.

Although the appearance of white settlers in black Africa has produced deep racial and social tensions, the impact of which were felt in all parts of Africa, European agricultural enterprise was actually restricted to limited areas of the African continent in relation to the vast land mass of Africa. Indeed, the disadvantages of tropical climate and disease in Africa plus the more attractive lands and opportunities in North and South America, Australia, and Russian Asia discouraged European immigration to Africa, and the great outpouring of Europeans to overseas territories in the nineteenth century by-passed Africa. European farmers thus confined their settlement to the temperate plateau country south of the Zambezi, or to healthy, fertile enclaves like the highlands of Kenya. European farming in Africa began at the Cape in the seventeenth century but remained restricted to the immediate hinterland. A dearth of capital and the availability of cheap, unskilled Hottentot and Bantu labor discouraged the immigration of Europeans to South Africa. The few whites who pressed into the dry highveld of the interior were cattlemen whose technological superiority enabled them to seize control of the land from the Bantu who remained after the depredations of the Mfecane. In a brief period most of the acreage available for agriculture passed to white ownership. Stimulated by the demand for agricultural products by the South African mining communities, and benefiting from the expanding communication, transportation, and financial facilities that accompanied the development of mining, South African farmers utilized new crops, methods, and mechanized equipment to become Africa's most prosperous exporters of agricultural products.

A similar process took place in the Rhodesias, where European settlers turned to farming after the anticipated gold rush never developed. Here they wrested the land from the Bantu peoples, supplied foodstuffs for the widely scattered mining communities, and utilized the railways and other facilities constructed to meet the needs of the miners. Nevertheless, farming in Southern Rhodesia remained unprofitable until the introduction of tobacco as a cash crop in the 1920s. With increasing capital the farmers could employ improved methods of cultivation and new agricultural techniques to obtain modest prosperity. The same pattern of white settlement in black Africa emerged in Kenya. Well-capitalized settlers from England and South African farmers fleeing from the aftereffects of the Anglo-Boer War settled in the fertile highlands of Kenya on unoccupied land traditionally belonging to the Kikuyu and utilized the facilities of the railway that linked Mombasa and Uganda. Unlike South Africa or Rhodesia, Kenya afforded European settlers little domestic market for food produce, since the colony possessed no industrial communities, and the settlers found prosperity only by developing tropical export crops like coffee, tea, sisal, and pyrethrum. Whether in South Africa, Rhodesia, or Kenya, pioneer farming entailed great hardship. Unknown plant and animal diseases frequently wiped out crops and herds. Markets were few, transportation uncertain, and capital scarce. Nevertheless, the European farmers prevailed, acquiring prosperity by mid-century, while developing specialized cash crops and new techniques previously unknown in traditional African farming.

Unhappily, these innovations have produced widespread social effects, the price of which, for many, has not been worth the economic advantages. Everywhere the white farmers settled, the black Africans lost control of the land and found themselves confined to smaller and less fertile regions than in precolonial times. Those who did not move to the reserves squatted on the European farms, creating an intractable and complex relationship between black African tenants and white European owners. Moreover, the European settlers frequently used their political power to extract economic concessions from the government and to defend their privileged social status to the detriment of both the few efficient large-scale white producers and the inefficient, but low-cost, African peasant producers. To be sure, the European farmers revolutionized agriculture in Africa wherever they settled and clearly stimulated African agricultural enterprise. The Africans were displaced from the land, but gained a security of person unknown in earlier periods of tribal conflicts; and, in many cases, the alienation of land was not permanent. The Africans were reduced in personal status and discriminated against, but they learned new techniques and acquired more efficient implements. Economic gains, however, hardly ever outweigh social and psychological losses. This was especially true in white-dominated Africa.

Although private business enterprise in Africa was largely confined to mining and railways, several large corporations—Unilever in the Congo and Firestone in Liberia—promoted large agricultural development schemes. In 1926 the Firestone Rubber Company received a vast concession from the Liberian government on extremely favorable terms. An independent African state surrounded by the territories of the colonial powers, Liberia was politically unstable and economically bankrupt. The Firestone concession resolved both these problems. Boundary disputes with France were settled and some of Liberia's debts were cleared. In the meantime, Firestone constructed a huge rubber plantation and became an employer, providing wages and previously unknown services for African laborers. Nevertheless, the presence of a powerful, profit-making concern in a weak and underdeveloped country produced inevitable tensions, antagonisms, and a host of new problems. The same accusations of exploitation leveled at the mining companies were charged against Firestone. The government of Liberia itself probably could not have acquired the capital or marshaled the organizational and technical talent required to launch a development scheme on the magnitude of the Firestone enterprise. Yet the manner and practice by which this enterprise was accomplished could only create tension between the Company and the economically weak and self-conscious African ruling group. Nevertheless, the African ruling group enthusiastically accepted the ends of the enterprise—economic development.

Without question, the most successful large-scale agricultural scheme in Africa was the exclusive product of neither private enterprise, nor of colonial administration, nor of peasant farmers, but rather it was the product of all three working together. Shortly after the reconquest of the Sudan in 1898, British officials began to consider the development of irrigated cotton in the Gezira, the island of land south of Khartoum between the Blue and the White Nile. Postponed at the outbreak of World War I, the project was revived in 1919. The Sudan government assumed responsibility for building the Sennar Dam and the major canals without which irrigation was impossible. A private corporation, the Sudan Plantations Syndicate, organized the scheme, provided the technical assistance needed, and marketed the crop. The tenants —about twenty-six thousand Sudanese peasant farmers—contributed the labor. The profits were divided 40 percent each for the government and the tenants and 20 percent for the Syndicate. Despite disease and the Depression, the Gezira Scheme was a dramatic economic success, and since World War II it has produced the capital to begin the modernization of the Sudan. Perhaps even more important, the Gezira Scheme combined the advantages of state ownership, the incentives and organizational skills of private enterprise, and the maintenance of a properous landed peasantry. To those prisoners of imperfect ideologies and impractical slogans, the Gezira Scheme demonstrated what can be accomplished in practice by utilizing the special advantages of government, business, and African farmers for mutual social and economic gain.

STATE AND SOCIETY

Ironically, the economic reasoning of European administrators in Africa was frequently indistinguishable from that of their socialist critics. Imperial officials believed that the state must control all facets of the economy to promote the general welfare; their African successors, whether civil servants or party politicians, have adopted the views of their former rulers. During the early decades of imperial administration, intervention by the state in the lives of African subjects at first remained limited to such rudimentary activities as order, taxation, and forced labor. European officials were few, and the Africans available to staff a bureaucracy were even fewer. Where possible, the colonial administration was, of necessity, required to rely on the hereditary authorities to assist in the task of ruling. As the growth of wealth in the individual territories made possible not only modernization but the bureaucracy to carry out that modernization, the degree of state intervention steadily increased. Such intervention introduced new patterns of living so that the traditional societies began to disintegrate, and the hereditary rulers steadily lost power to the educated African elite who, as minor officials in the colonial administration, had come to learn and to use the state machinery and, later, as politicians, to control it. Like European officials, the African elite were prepared to use the power of the state to press modernization forward and, of course, to advance their own positions and interests. Although the African elite have justified state control by a host of ideologies ranging from European socialism to traditional African communalism, the dominant role of the state in society is perhaps the most pervasive legacy of European imperial rule.

Next to the imposition of colonial rule itself, the most direct form of government intervention in the lives of African subjects was the recruitment and use of compulsory labor. Western beliefs in the virtues of work along with the economic needs of European settlers, mine owners, and officials for labor overcame the humanitarian scruples of imperial administrators and convinced them that the African had to be made to work for his own good and for that of the state. Unhappily, forced labor was frequently characterized by brutalities. Moreover, it was inefficient since the Africans had little incentive to work and discovered many ways to avoid service. The very presence of large numbers of cheap laborers dragooned and organized to work tended to discourage the introduction of labor-saving devices. Gradually, however, colonial authorities came to realize that the African is not idle, lazy, and immoral, but like all men is susceptible to economic incentives. As the machinery of colonial government evolved, the need for compulsory labor diminished, and the appearance of railways and truck transport made the conscripted carrier an anachronism. Thus, a combination of economic realities and humanitarian concern ended compulsion in British territories after World War I and in the French colonies after World War II, although Portugal did not officially abandon forced labor until 1957. The disappearance of compulsory labor in Africa did not, however, mean a decrease in state interference in African society, for forced labor was only abandoned when the colonial administrators had developed a bureaucracy that, in fact, imposed greater, rather than less, control over the individual African.

Just as the increase in revenue enabled the colonial government to assert its authority, World War I provided new opportunities to expand state control. In order to mobilize the war effort in Africa between 1914 and 1918, particularly in East Africa, both the British and German administrators recruited Africans for military service, labor, and porterage. Even in those territories unaffected by actual combat, the imperial officials peremptorily organized the human and material resources of the colony to support the wider Allied war effort. The effectiveness of this effort was directly proportional to the number of administrators and the cooperation of the traditional authorities.

The role of the imperial administration in African life rapidly increased throughout colonial Africa before and after World War II. Postwar prosperity made the extension of administration possible, but the enthusiasm for colonial development completely eclipsed the nineteenth-century idea that the colonies must pay the cost of their own administration and development. There was a widespread belief that the states should mobilize African resources for development in peacetime just as the state had to mobilize colonial resources for war. Only by rapid economic development could the conditions of the African peoples be improved, and such modernization could only be accomplished by the direct use of the state machinery, both colonial and metropolitan. The enthusiasm of colonial officials for state planning and production in postwar Africa, matched in the past only by the moral fervor of Christian evangelists, was strongly supported by the African nationalists and those European socialists who came to power at the end of the war. Thus, the Labor party in Britain inaugurated the Tanganyika peanut project designed to produce peanuts for oil through a vast, mechanized agricultural scheme. Despite millions of pounds and millions of acres, the planners made many mistakes, and by 1950 they realized that large-scale mechanical production of peanuts was not economically possible. The dismal failure of the Tanganyika peanut project once again demonstrated that giant, centralized government cultivation schemes were not necessarily the answer to agricultural development in Africa. The African peasant farmer had demonstrated in Nigeria, Ghana, Senegal, Uganda, and the Sudan that he not only reacted positively to economic incentives, but was sufficiently adaptable to fluctuations in local conditions. With technical advice and government assistance the peasant was capable of producing cash crops and eager to improve his standard of living. In many regions of Africa the combination of peasant farmers working small plots with government aid was both more productive and more efficient than large schemes involving central planning, huge public expenditure, and massive mechanization.

The control of foreign trade by colonial administrations had an even greater impact upon African subjects than government participation in agriculture and industry. Foreign trade affected all those individuals who were involved in the market economy. The manipulation of the economy by the imperial authorities, which was frequently for the benefit of the metropolitan power, directly affected African standards of living. Although the French had always been protectionist, the British African empire had been built in the nineteenth century on the principles of free trade. The Great Depression ended this long tradition, but it was not until World War II that a massive system of trade restrictions and currency control was imposed on the colonies. The elaborate machinery of export monopolies, licensing, currency regulations, and price fixing were not only continued after the war, but were extended and made more effective. Thus, powerful marketing boards were created with full authority to purchase African crops and to sell them abroad. By determining the price paid to African farmers for their crops, these marketing boards accumulated large reserves, which were spent on public works rather than returned as profit to the peasant producers. The policies of the marketing boards, in fact, amounted to a form of heavy indirect taxation upon the peasantry.

The marketing boards combined the attitudes of the most conservative, paternalistic colonial official with the socialist belief in the virtues of state planning. Both had little faith in the African, thinking that he would only squander his cash, thereby producing inflation, parasitic middlemen, and crops of inferior quality. The boards developed into a large, inflexible bureaucracy staffed by overpaid and undertaxed officials, both European and African, who had ample opportunities for graft and bribery. More important, the monopolistic power of the boards forced peasants to be increasingly dependent upon the state and its agents, who frequently could not separate their economic role from politics. Created by imperial administrators, the system not only taxed the peasant and discouraged the growth of an African mercantile middle class, but it provided an organization for the manipulation of the territory's economy to the metropolitan rulers' advantage and for the distribution of political patronage by their African successors.

EDUCATION   If Europeans controlled the economies of their African colonies, they also introduced Western education, which produced an ineradicable impression on the minds of Africans. The Christian missionaries were the first Europeans who consciously attempted to transform African ways of thought, and consequently, they played a major role in the great social revolution produced by European imperialism in Africa. In many parts of Africa missionaries had preceded the partition and occupation by the colonial powers. Fundamentally, they represented a new way of life in which the individual and his relation to God, his means of livelihood, and his wife and family would take primacy over traditional beliefs in ancestral spirits, primitive methods of subsistence, extended kinships, and polygamy. The Christian life could only be introduced to the African through Western education and example, and thus the preaching of the Christian faith required the creation of schools and hospitals as adjuncts of the Church. In the effort to impart a new faith, the missionaries had to make their converts literate, thereby opening to them the vast world of Western learning, which far transcended knowledge of the Christian religion. Throughout the colonies bush schools were built in which African catechists passed on the rudiments of reading, writing, and arithmetic; from there a few students went on to more advanced boarding schools.

Despite the devotion of white and black missionaries, however, the missions were never able to mount a massive program of education. The European and American missionary societies were supported by volunteer contributions that were never sufficient. In the early years many missionaries died from disease, limiting the work of evangelization and education. Frequently, the missions overextended their commitments in order to forestall competition, and at times they ignored both the faith and education in unseemly struggles with rival Christian sects. Moreover, by advocating a new way of life, they not only had to face hostility from the traditional African religious and secular leaders, but in the early years were virtually ostracized by African society and had to depend upon orphans and outcasts for converts. Later, when Africans began to attend mission schools in greater numbers as the value of Western education became more apparent and demonstrable, most Africans clearly wanted literacy first and Christianity second, accepting religious instruction as the price one had to pay for secular learning. The missionary priorities were, of course, exactly opposite, and this frequently produced tensions between missionary teachers and pupil converts. But the missionaries were not free from state supervision. Whatever their religious affiliations, most colonial officials regarded the missionaries with deep suspicion. The same paternal attitudes that led European officials to intervene in the economic and social life of the Africans also acted to protect them from overzealous missionaries. In the Southern Sudan the government arbitrarily assigned rival mission societies to spheres with boundaries that could not be violated, in order to prevent religious rivalry, if not religious wars, such as that which devastated Uganda before the imposition of British rule. In other regions, particularly Northern Nigeria and the Northern Sudan, Christian missionaries were purposely excluded to avoid antagonizing the predominantly Muslim population. The result was a bitter legacy of states divided religiously as well as racially.

Although the missionaries demonstrated the value of the new learning and created a new class of literate Africans whö saw that education meant prestige and privilege, the great mass of the population was left untouched by mission work. The schools were few, the syllabuses irrelevant, and the local environment ill-suited to encourage the children of peasants to attend the mission. The few who did attend usually dropped out to meet parental demands in the homestead or could not afford the school fees. There were not many converts other than the literate few. There were, to be sure, many sincere converts, but most Africans did not totally abandon their traditional beliefs. Frequently, Africans incorporated Biblical examples in their religious practices. At times they used Christian liturgy to express resentment against the colonial order, and they rarely surrendered belief in the ancestral spirits and resisted mission teachings on polygamy, pagan ritual, and other Christian sins.

After World War I financial support for African missions began to dwindle, and the missionaries were increasingly willing to receive government support in order to continue and expand their educational and, concomitantly, their evangelical work. At the same time colonial officials displayed greater willingness to provide educational subsidies. Not only had the colonial economies grown sufficiently to produce greater revenues for education, but by utilizing the facilities and teachers of the established missions, the imperial administration could provide education cheaply. Moreover, if the government helped pay for mission education, it could insist upon certain standards and courses of instruction to train Africans more effectively for the lower echelons of the growing bureaucracy. The creeping paternalism of colonial administration was thus extended with few difficulties to education.

Once involved in the complex task of education, the imperial officials were faced with the problem of defining their objectives and justifying their educational philosophies. The French concentrated on educating a small Gallicized elite who were assimilated by mastering the French language, history, and culture. The Portuguese adopted similar objectives but included religious instruction as an integral part of the curriculum. The Belgians were more practical. They made little effort to create a highly educated Europeanized intellectual elite, preferring to give the rudiments of literacy to many at the primary level so that large numbers of Africans could acquire industrial and vocational training to serve the economic development of the Congo. The British were even more pragmatic and devolutionary. Each colony was permitted to formulate its own policy, but unlike the French and Belgians, the British stressed those aspe of local life and African values that did not con with British humanitarian and moral precepts. mary education was carried out in the vernacular African languages. Nevertheless, in all the British territories, particularly in West Africa, a considerable number of Africans passed beyond the primary school to institutions of higher education, where they became thoroughly Anglicized.

Differences in educational policy should not obscure fundamental similarities in African education throughout the continent. After World War II, education, particularly primary education, greatly expanded everywhere. European languages became widely known, and as literacy increased, made possible the introduction of new ideas, including those criticisms of the colonial administration that appeared in the African press, which catered to the growing literate class. Education acquired prestige. Not only did the educated have more and better opportunities, but they were respected. From their ranks came the leaders for national independence.

Secondary and university education grew more slowly and selectively than did primary schooling and accounted for a minor percentage of the total school population. The increased costs of higher education prohibited rapid expansion, and in many territories the more conservative officials were highly suspicious of well-educated Africans. To them, the purpose of education was to train Africans for the convenience of the administration, which required literate Africans for minor posts and offices. They did not favor Africans having education equal or superior to their own, enabling them to criticize and challenge colonial rule and to be troublesome within the otherwise placid structure of colonial decision making.

Like primary schools, institutions of higher learning began under religious auspices and were expected to train African ministers. Thus, the Church Missionary Society founded Fourah Bay College in Sierra Leone as early as 1827. Development of secular colleges did not really begin until after World War I. By necessity and design these institutions were small, and they accommodated only a few students so that many more Africans went abroad, particularly to Europe and the United States, for higher education. After World War II the British provided large sums to expand the existing universities and to create new ones. At the same time that the empire was diminishing, the demand for European higher education in Africa was rapidly increasing.

All the African universities owe their beginnings to Europeans and were European in curriculum, control, and academic traditions. For a long time the faculty was dominated by European instructors who were determined to preserve Western standards of scholarship and salaries. Not surprisingly, they transferred to Africa the courses of study they were accustomed to in Europe. As in Europe, they emphasized quality rather than quantity so that an intellectual elite, who had little in common with the mass of Africans, was created. Even when European teachers sought to introduce African-oriented courses, the Africans were frequently reluctant to accept them. They regarded the teaching of such courses as an attempt to provide education inferior to that of Europe and as an attempt to delay African development toward independence. Most African graduates sought careers in the civil service or politics. The fact that most African students continued their higher education on government scholarships unintentionally helped to confirm their belief in the importance of the state in every sphere of life. Nevertheless, within half a century Western education had produced a literate class with the capabilities to challenge European rule and, ultimately, to win independence. Although frequently branded as cultural imperialism, the educational revolution in Africa has been dramatically expanded by every independent African state whose leaders, whatever their political views, have repeatedly pledged their deep commitment to education by allocating increasing percentages of their limited resources to schooling at all levels.

MEDICINE   Perhaps the most successful application of Western education has been the development and use of tropical medicine. Africa is a continent plagued by a host of debilitating and deadly diseases. Before the coming of the Europeans, the treatment of disease was in the hands of medicinemen who often combined healing with ritual functions. Despite a shrewd and skillful knowledge of herbs and medicinal plants, the African medicine man had no effective remedies for malaria, sleeping sickness, bilharziasis, leprosy, typhoid, or meningitis, to name but a few of Africa's terrible diseases, and even today disease in Africa is the chief reason for a life expectancy of only about thirty-five years. Moreover, the incomers, Europeans and Asians, introduced new diseases, such as smallpox, against which the Africans had little natural resistance.

As in education, the first Europeans to deal with tropical disease were mission doctors who, like their pedagogical counterparts, used medicine as a means of evangelization. They had, however, only limited success commensurate with their restricted human and financial resources. Thus, the great assault on tropical disease was launched by the colonial governments as a foundation for social progress. Their success was made possible by the enormous increase in medical knowledge in Europe during the twentieth century and the administrative control in Africa, which enabled doctors to apply it. Humanitarian pressure from home plus the paternalism of European officials and the self-interest of mine owners and settlers in Africa, who understood the advantages to be gained from healthy workers, led to the inauguration of schemes of preventive medicine and public health.

The development of health services in Africa closely paralleled that in education and was a direct reflection of the economic resources of the colony and the increasing aid from Europe after World War II. Gradually, a network of hospitals, clinics, and dispensaries was constructed in each colony, which usually emanated from a central hospital in the capital or large cities, where the more complicated cases were treated, and terminated with bush dispensaries in the rural villages. These dispensaries were usually staffed with Africans whose medical education was limited to special courses conducted at the central hospitals, but whose experience often made them skilled diagnosticians. With the growth of educational facilities, more Africans were sent to Europe for medical training, and in most colonies, medical schools formed a bridge between the new colleges and the central hospitals in the cities. As in education, the emphasis was on quality, not quantity, and the number of African doctors remained few in relation to the need. In Africa as well as in Europe doctors working in schools of tropical medicine sought to understand and then to find cures for the individual diseases. One by one new methods of treatment and more effective drugs were developed to combat disease. The application of this knowledge was more difficult, however, depending on the resources and organization of the colonies' medical services to carry out preventive and curative medicine in the towns and countryside.

The social and political effects of the campaign against tropical disease were far-reaching but are difficult to assess. Clearly, the death rate declined and the life expectancy of the African increased. Under European rule the African birthrate rose dramatically, and in some territories the population even doubled. The economic, political, and social impact of this population increase is as perplexing as it is controversial, but no one can dispute the fact that the introduction and implementation of tropical medicine were the greatest contribution of Europeans to Africa.

CITIES   The prevention and cure of disease became especially critical with the rise of new cities and the expansion of traditional urban settlements in Africa. African cities have existed since ancient times, and the great walled commercial towns of the Sudan and East Africa astonished the first Europeans to visit them. Nevertheless, the number of inhabitants in towns like Timbuktu, Kano, and Mombasa remained limited, since even the most productive African societies possessed insufficient food surpluses to sustain a large urban population, and the difficulties of communication and transportation discouraged peasants from traveling to the towns. Such obstacles were largely overcome by the use of European technology. Improved means of transportation made possible the rapid movement of people, goods, and food. Health services counteracted the problems of communicable diseases in a congested environment. European methods and materials created new architecture and standards of construction. Town planning enabled the Europeans to impose new techniques of organization and administration. In virtually every colony there was a rapid expansion of urban settlement around old trading centers such as Dakar, mining communities such as Johannesburg, and administrative headquarters such as Lusaka, Nairobi, and Leopoldville.

Although each European-built city differed dramatically in its location, purpose, and appearance, they all possessed two common characteristics: they had been built where nothing had previously existed and they were all very recent creations. Their rapid expansion was the result of thousands of rural Africans flocking to the cities, where the number of Africans far exceeded the number of jobs and houses. Too many people and too little work produced a large unemployed urban population huddled in shanty towns that sprang up overnight on the peripheries of the cities, where municipal services—lighting, sanitation, social welfare—were limited or nonexistent. Although poverty was eased by newcomers moving in with their wealthier and more established kinsmen, life in the shanty towns was hard, unhappy, and frequently short.

Like the white official who lived in temporary comfort during his tour of duty, only to retire to London or Paris, the African town dweller vacillated between his ancestral fields in the countryside and his home in the city, having neither commitment nor a sense of belonging to either. The social instability created by those who wandered from city to country and back again increased the tensions of unemployment and alienation in the urban environment. Several colonial governments, particularly Rhodesia, South Africa, and the Congo, sought to restrain the rush to the towns by imposing controls through an elaborate system of passes designed to restrict the movements of Africans and to keep them in the rural reserves. Those Africans who reached the city were required to live in strictly segregated residential areas. In the settler colonies the whites argued that the city was a European creation in which the African was but a temporary laborer permitted to reside by white sufferance. He was not allowed the presumption to live with the whites. In fact, residential segregation was not peculiar to colonial cities, for the walled towns of West Africa had traditionally been partitioned into ethnic quarters, nor was there much opposition to segregation in the early years of European rule, when the economic and social differences between Europe and Africa were apparent and accepted. With the creation of a Western-educated elite possessing middle-class incomes and social standards, however, residential segregation became a bitter grievance. The African professional class resented being confined to areas inhabited by illiterate African laborers, and they were exasperated to discover that they could not freely invest their newly acquired wealth in real estate.

The social tensions produced by this form of European exploitation were further exacerbated by the fact that status, class, and privilege no longer counted for much in the hostile leveling process of the urban environment. There was little with which the African, or the white immigrant for that matter, could identify, so the city failed to produce much civic pride or to create a sense of belonging to a community. Yet despite the tensions, hostility, and exploitation, the new cities of Africa offered excitement, entertainment, and opportunity. Crime, vice, and slums flourished, but the relief from the tedium of rural life, the pleasure of anonymity, and even the slum dwellings themselves, which in many ways were superior to the wattle and daub huts of the village, acted as a powerful magnet, irresistibly drawing the Africans out of the countryside. Once in the city the new townsmen were confronted by a host of new organizations, new standards of conduct, and better services. In the bubbling cauldron of the African city, ideas, rumors, and opinions circulated with unbelievable rapidity, carried by a host of magazines, newspapers, and radios, unknown in the rural areas. In the city, the political parties were founded through which the new political ideas that were conceived in the school, the marketplace, and the party headquarters were absorbed and propagated, and they flourished in the free climate of the towns. In the city, independent Africa was nurtured.

Chapter 5

Dismantling
the Empires

World War II precipitated dramatic and rapid
changes in European imperialism in Africa. In 1939
all of Africa was under European rule, except Liberia,
which was dominated by the Firestone Rubber Company. Even the redoubtable Ethiopians had capitulated
before the Italians determined to revenge the humilia-
tion of Aduwa. Moreover, European control appeared
everywhere too strong to challenge, and even African
resistance had submerged beneath the steady, unhur-
ried pace of change in colonial Africa. In fact, European technological innovations in the twentieth century had seemed to secure indefinite European rule in
Africa. True, the idea of trusteeship that had matured
after World War I implied future self-government,
but at a time so remote that hardly anyone seriously
envisaged an independent Africa in the twentieth century. World War II destroyed these assumptions.

IMPACT OF
WORLD WAR II

For over half a century Europeans had been able to
dominate Africans not only because of their superior
military, economic, and technical resources, but also
because of the self-confidence with which they ruled.
The belief in European invincibility was not confined
to the imperialists. Most Africans were convinced that
the white man was superior. World War II shattered

this illusion. The Japanese overran the southeast Asian empires of Britain, France, and the Netherlands with humiliating ease. The Italians once again were driven from Ethiopia, and the French were not only disastrously defeated by German armies, but the dissension and infighting that followed between the Free French and the puppet Vichy government only illuminated French weakness.

The appearance in Africa of European and American troops had a profound impact on those Africans who came in contact with them, for these soldiers behaved very differently from the aloof and imperious colonial officials to whom the Africans were accustomed. Conversely, thousands of African troops were recruited by Britain and France and served in Ethiopia, North Africa and overseas in Asia and Europe; there they not only gained a perspective by which to measure their own societies in Africa, but by killing white men and by making friendships with white women in Europe, they learned that the white rulers in Africa were not invincible. Throughout all of Africa the colonial powers lost enormous prestige that could never be regained, and the psychological attitudes of the rulers and the ruled toward one another altered dramatically. The colonial officials lost their self-confidence. The Africans regained theirs. The imperial tradition was dying and the possibility of an independent Africa was born.

Despite the ultimate victory of Britain and France in World War II, events during the immediate postwar years undermined, rather than strengthened, the position of the colonial powers. In 1948 Great Britain dismantled her great Indian empire, and the subcontinent was partitioned between India and Pakistan. Ceylon became independent, followed by Burma. The independence of south Asia not only established a precedent for the liberation of colonial peoples elsewhere, but produced four powerful states pledged to free dependent peoples everywhere from European control. The imperial powers did not, however, regard the granting of independence to the south Asian states as a revolutionary precedent. In 1941 President Roosevelt and Prime Minister Winston Churchill met on a battleship off the Atlantic coast and signed the Atlantic Charter in which they declared the "right of all peoples to choose the form of government under which they will live." Although Churchill later qualified the sweeping terms of the Charter to exclude the colonies of the British empire from the right of self-determination, many politically conscious peoples in Africa and Asia never forgot the appeals of the Charter or that Churchill had not intended it to apply to them.

The French were even more adamant than the British in their determination to maintain the integrity of their empire, and the creation of the French Union, in which all subjects became French citizens, appeared an ill-disguised substitute for the old empire against which Ho Chi Minh and his Communist guerrillas successfully fought to free Indochina. The partition of Indochina into three independent states was preceded by the independence of Indonesia from the Dutch. Although none of these struggles directly affected Africa, they gave inspiration to African nationalists and confirmed the imperial weaknesses of European nations first exposed by World War II.

Added to the defeats and liquidation of European empire in Asia was the decisive influence of the United States, Russia, and the United Nations in the evolution of the African and Asian independence movements. World War II had shifted the balance of power away from the European center to the periphery, where the two superstates—the United States and Russia—possessed predominate economic and military power. Both the United States and Russia had anticolonial traditions, the former rooted in the reality and myths of her own War of Independence, the latter the product of Communist ideology. Despite the fact that both the United States and Russia have since violated these traditions, the influence of these two immensely powerful states was crucial. The Russians operated more through the Communist states, who at that time were either satellites or willing allies in the struggle against capitalism. The United States exerted its influence largely through the United Nations, which was founded in 1945. The successor to the League of Nations, the United Nations assumed the supervision of the former mandated territories, except for South-West Africa. In that territory the government of South Africa refused to transfer jurisdiction to the United Nations and continues to this day to administer it. More important, the Charter of the United Nations Organization contained, largely because of American pressure, a statement of the rights of all peoples to freedom and justice, the obvious implications of which were as repugnant to the colonial powers as they were welcomed by Afro-Asian nationalists. Moreover, the independence of the new Asian states and their admission into the United Nations instantly altered the composition of the General Assembly so that a bloc of smaller powers, many of them former colonies, now became vociferous in their insistence on a rapid end to colonialism throughout the world.

The determination of these Asian states was dramatically demonstrated by the conference held at Bandung in Indonesia in 1955. Although the Africans played only a peripheral role, mainly as observers, the major purpose of the conference—to end colonialism in all its manifestations—was not lost on the Africans. The sense of solidarity, the sympathy, and the precedent established by the Bandung Conference provided great support for African nationalists in their efforts to end European imperial rule in Africa.

POSTWAR ECONOMIC DEVELOPMENT

While African nationalists were encouraged to organize for independence, European rulers in Africa were not idle. When African nationalists were seeking to dismantle European control, the colonial governments were more innovative than at any time during their half-century of administration. In one sense this burst of activity was simply the fruition of slow, but steady, development. During the early decades after the occupation of Africa, colonial administrations were required to be virtually self-supporting. In the interwar period what little extra moneys had become available for education, health, and social services were soon wiped out by the Depression. World War II, however, brought new prosperity. The insatiable European demand for raw materials when Europe could not pay for them in manufactured goods produced large credit balances in many of the African colonies. Moreover, these credits were controlled by the colonial governments, which had, through marketing boards, bought crops at fixed prices and then sold them on the world market at higher prices. Of course, the individual grower lost the difference and certainly received little incentive to expand production or to use his profits for other enterprises. Nevertheless, the colonial governments suddenly found themselves in possession of sufficient funds to enable the implementation of large-scale development schemes for the general welfare. This authoritarian control of the economy not only contributed to the growth of socialism at the expense of the budding entrepreneurial class, but it convinced many educated Africans who were recruited to staff the growing bureaucracy that only the state could resolve the social and economic problems of modernization.

Just as the funds available from the internal resources of the colony increased after World War II, colonial administrations were now able to acquire large sums from their home governments—sums that had been unobtainable in the past, either for ideological or practical reasons. This was made possible by a variety of complex, interlocking considerations, not least of which was the rather mundane mechanism developed by European governments during the war to tax a much larger proportion of the personal and corporate income of their citizens. After the war these high levels of taxation were maintained so that Western governments could operate with greatly increased revenues. These revenues were spent on social services —health, education, housing, pensions, unemployment insurance—and on defense, but from the vast sums available the home governments did allocate a small share of the total for development schemes in the colonies. New attitudes toward colonial finance, which had been evolving in the interwar period, now reached fruition. The ideology of the welfare state at home—that the more fortunate should help the less fortunate—found its counterpart overseas in the ideology of trusteeship. Just as laissez-faire economics died in Europe, so, too, did the assumption that African colonies must be self-sufficient and should not be a burden on the mother country. The cynic usually attributed this change in attitude to the white man's guilt; the humanitarian called it the triumph of morality. More practical men reasoned that in an age of decolonization former colonies would be of greater use to Europe if their economies could be sufficiently developed to sustain independence rather than left stagnant and helpless in the world of predatory nation-states. As is usually the case, the wisdom of practical men has proved more durable than the pronouncements of the humanitarians or the disparaging sarcasm of the misanthrope.

The new philosophy of economic development in Africa was translated into hard reality by the succession of Colonial Development and Welfare Acts passed by the British Parliament and their French counterpart, the Investment Fund for Economic and Social Development (Fonds d'Investissement pour le Développement Economique et Social, or FIDES) approved by the French Chamber of Deputies. Between 1946 and 1955 Britain provided £210 million for development schemes in British territories, while the French poured francs from FIDES into Africa at an even greater rate. By far the most spectacular projects were the plethora of hydroelectric schemes at Jinja on the Nile, at Kariba on the Zambezi, the Volta River dam at Akasombo, and at Fria and Kimbo in Guinea—all designed to provide power for industrialization. Less dramatic but equally significant efforts were made in agriculture, education, and local government.

Despite the prospect of industrialization powered by these hydroelectric schemes, Africa would clearly remain dependent upon its agricultural production for many decades, and in every colony efforts were made to increase and diversify agricultural production, not only in cash crops, but also in traditional foodstuffs to feed the rapidly expanding towns. In every colony, agricultural and veterinary services were extended into even the most remote districts. Despite the frequent reluctance of farmers to employ new techniques, great efforts were made to educate them and to introduce better tools and machines. Cooperatives and modest agricultural schemes were inaugurated in order to consolidate petty plots and to take advantage of technical innovations and the improvements in soil fertility. Among the pastoralists, similar efforts were undertaken by veterinary teams to improve breeds and to concentrate on raising animals for quality and not simply quantity. All these activities in the rural areas would have been of little value if the farmers could not have gotten the new produce to markets, so during the decade following World War II an ever-increasing proportion of development budgets was invested in improving roads and transport facilities as a basic requirement for further modernization.

EXPANSION OF EDUCATION

Education also consumed a large proportion of development funds. Development schemes cost money and require highly educated and skilled personnel to carry them out. At the end of World War II there was a dearth of educated people in every African territory and, consequently, large numbers of Europeans had to be recruited to carry out the plans for development. Unfortunately, the new Europeans were expensive; their high salaries, houses, and free travel consumed alarming amounts of the moneys set aside for personnel. More deplorable were the political and social repercussions from this new influx of European invaders in Africa. Because they had skills, they were frequently arrogant toward those Africans who did not possess similar technical training, or they downgraded the few who did. Unlike the imperial officials, they had little knowledge of the colony or its people and cared less. Unlike European administrators, they had no long-term commitment to the colonies. They came to perform specific tasks to collect their salaries, and to return to Europe. Rapid modernization in Africa could not have been undertaken without them, but they increased the alienation between the Europeans and Africans, and by their very numbers, let alone their social assumptions, created the impression that the colonial powers were increasing, not devolving, their control of Africa. It is little wonder that education for the Africans was the basic requirement for the economic, political, and social development of Africa by the Africans.

The expansion of education in the postwar period was inaugurated by the colonial governments themselves and concentrated on secondary schools, teacher-training centers, and university colleges. In the past, Western education in Africa had been largely in the hands of missionaries and confined to primary education. Clearly, both the resources and curricula were patently inadequate to train Africans to carry out schemes of modernization. Therefore, primary education was reformed and extended from four to six years. Secondary schools were established and staffed with instructors brought from Europe and the few Africans who had graduated from the existing schools. At the same time, university colleges were established; in 1945 alone four were founded—Ibadan in Nigeria, Khartoum in the Sudan, Achimota on the Gold Coast, and Makerere in Uganda. In the French territories an ever-increasing number of Africans was sent to France for university and technical training. Despite the commitment, however, elaborate systems of secondary and higher education could not be constructed overnight. There is no such thing as an "instant university," and even the best intentions failed to produce a sufficient number of educated personnel to staff the burgeoning bureaucratic agencies created by the new prosperity. The failure was caused by poor planning and was not an effort by British and French officials to retard decolonization deliberately. Their efforts to press forward in good faith with educational development, even when the results were meager, was in striking contrast to the efforts of the Belgians and the Portuguese, to whom secondary and higher education seemed economically unnecessary and politically unwise in colonies that were planned to remain under European control for a long time to come.

Accompanying economic and educational expansion was a corresponding growth in local government. Indirect rule, the cornerstone of British policy in colonial Africa, was quietly abandoned. Even its most ardent supporters realized that there was no longer sufficient time for African institutions to evolve along their own lines. The alternative chosen was to impose upon African societies European models of local government, usually consisting of elected councils presided over by a chief. These councils were then given responsibility for those local services that had hitherto been supervised by the chief or the district commissioner. The English county council formed the model for most British territories; the French commune, the unit of local government in France, was introduced into the French colonies. Although the councils frequently failed to function and were almost never as efficient as those administrations headed by European district officers, they provided administrative responsibility for Africans whose lack of education disqualified them from the civil service, and they provided a means of political training for future national politicians.

At the state level the imperialists displayed ambiguities and contradictions in the creation of national representative institutions; although they were not as apparent at the local level, these contradictions and ambiguities caused the British and the French to lose the initiative to African nationalist movements. The British sought to repeat in Africa the pattern of constitutional development that had evolved in Canada and Australia; political power was to be conferred upon a legislative assembly or council with at first an "official" majority of senior government officials. Gradually, a "non-official" African representation was to be added, first with Africans nominated by British governors and later with representatives elected by an ever-increasing electorate, until the assembly became, in fact, controlled by an elected African majority. A similar process would take place in the executive branch. In each colony the governor was the chief executive officer assisted by an executive council. Gradually, representation was granted to non-officials, including Africans, so that the executive councils evolved into cabinets, the ministers of which were dependent upon a majority in the legislative council. The success of this traditional pattern of constitutional change varied from one colony to another.

In West Africa, where British officials, teachers, and technicians were temporary residents, few obstacles appeared in the evolution of the legislative and executive councils. In East and Central Africa, however, lived white settlers who regarded themselves not only as permanent residents, but residents who rightfully possessed numerous social, economic, and political privileges. The granting of the franchise to the African majorities in these territories threatened to strip the white settlers of their privileged political position and to jeopardize their social standing and economic power. Here the evolution of national representative institutions faced the tortuous contradiction of British policy, as the imperial government sought to protect the settlers from a too rapid transfer of power to African majorities, on the one hand, and attempted to satisfy the demands of the Africans for greater representation, on the other. Thus, for over a decade the British experimented with multiracial constitutions in which seats were allotted to interests, not persons, much like the French Estates General of the *ancien régime*, so that all groups would be represented in relation to their position in society. Africans inculcated by Western education to associate democracy with "one man-one vote" regarded these multiracial constitutions as a sham, and in the end the British could not overcome this inherent contradiction. Ultimately, African majorities gained control of all British legislative councils north of the Zambezi. But the failure of the multiracial constitutions to survive should not obscure the fact that they provided a transitional stage without which no accommodation could have been made between white-settler minorities and black-African majorities.

French constitutional development proved even more contradictory, the product of two conflicting traditions in the history of modern France itself. By creating a centralized imperial system within which the Africans would have local autonomy, the French sought to resolve the struggle between the tradition of identity, by which all Africans would be French citizens, and the tradition of paternalism, by which the Africans would be French subjects. Represented at first by the French Union and then by the French Community, the attempt to keep the colonies closely tied to France tended to retard the development of territorial assemblies within the colonies. The powers of these assemblies remained considerably less than the British legislative councils—they could not debate political subjects, for instance—and the French administration continued to function independently and paternalistically. Nevertheless, these assemblies allowed French Africans to enjoy more influence than in the past and, like their counterparts in British Africa, they gained political experience and a territorial identity with which to challenge the domination of France and its imperial system.

Whereas both the British and the French sought to create representative institutions at the national level, the Portuguese and the Belgians did not. One could hardly expect a dictatorship in Portugal to embark upon democratic experiments in Africa. The Belgians, preoccupied with economic development of the Congo, gave little thought to political evolution at either the local or national levels. Ultimately this produced disastrous results. Certainly, the efforts of the British and the French were better than those of the Portuguese and the Belgians. While the increasing dependence of the British and French on European models may be understandable, it frequently did not adapt to the realities of African nationalism and confused the African politicians who were expected to operate these alien institutions.

AFRICAN
NATIONALISM

The origins of African nationalism are to be found in the early resistance movements and in the doubts of the first mission-educated Africans in the beginning years of colonialism. Later, Africans who went overseas in the interwar years to acquire a higher education that was unavailable in Africa were exposed to new experiences and ideologies, which they brought back to Africa in their intellectual baggage. In America Africans discovered a modern state that had broken the chains of colonialism. Even more significant was the search for identity by many of the American blacks who, although long resident in the New World, still looked to Africa as their mystical homeland to which they were linked by the color of their skin. This deep racial consciousness was expressed in the mid-nineteenth century by Edward Blyden as "the African personality," and variations of this theme were later enunciated in political terms by Marcus Garvey as "Africa for the Africans" and in wider terms by the Pan-Africanism of William Du Bois. Fashioned for the most part in America by American blacks, these ideas and the movement they sustained were taken up by Africans in the 1940s and merged with the ideologies of socialism and communism, which the Africans educated in Europe had readily accepted. Although communism has never attracted many Africans, the anti-imperialism, humanitarian goals, and communal ownership of socialism did. After being altered to fit the realities and needs of Africa, these two ideologies, Pan-Africanism from America and socialism from Europe, became the twin pillars of African nationalism.

While nationalism among English-speaking Africans was concerned with winning the political kingdom, nationalism among French-speaking Africans focused at first upon cultural, rather than political, values. Clearly, the Pan-Africanism of Du Bois asserted the values of African culture, but as part of a political movement. The need for an affirmation of cultural values before political action could be successful was persuasively argued by the Senegalese poet and politician, Léopold Senghor, and the West Indian

Aimé Cesaire, who formulated the concept of *Négritude*. Under the pervasive influence of Senghor, many young French West Africans turned more to the rediscovery and renewal of African culture and history, usually expressed in French. The emphasis on cultural values meant that political consciousness in these territories evolved more slowly than in British Africa, and demands for independence from France remained more hesitant and ambiguous.

Neither intellectual speculation on the uniqueness of the African personality nor the search for a cultural identity in the African past and present could have, by themselves, produced decolonization and independence in Africa. The educated African elite who were stimulated by these ideas were relatively few in number and invariably alienated from the masses, without whose support the nationalists could hardly have challenged European control successfully. The incorporation of African peasants and townsmen into the nationalist movement was accomplished by the organization of national congresses and political parties. These political organizations were, in fact, the products of earlier African associations, particularly in West Africa, which had been formed in the early years of colonialism for educational, cultural, or recreational purposes. The influence and size of such organizations were limited, however, to a few towns and to middle-class Africans who had education and wealth.

After World War II national congresses were organized in an effort to secure wider support than the earlier welfare associations had gained or, in fact, had sought. Inspired largely by the example of the Indian Congress party, these congresses were the direct result of the worldwide political unrest that the war had produced. Claiming to speak for all the people, the congress in each territory was loosely organized around a nucleus of nationalists. Perpetually short of funds, they were invariably unable to discipline the many rival groups and competing interests within the organization. The emphasis was more on action than programs, and they sought to assert themselves by boycotts, strikes, and civil disobedience. In the 1950s political parties began to evolve from the interest groups within the congresses and soon secured the initiative in the struggle for independence. Better organized and disciplined than the congress, the political party was the work of a new generation of politicians that was more militant, more impatient, and more "African." Confident of their own strength, they relied less on the European liberals and socialists and emphasized that the independence movement was uniquely African. Men like Kwame Nkrumah and Léopold Senghor replaced their more moderate elders. They demanded constitutional reform and the vote, and as they gradually received both, the political parties attracted a mass following, which was a formidable challenge to the colonial administration. Some African politicians made extravagant promises; others appealed to tribal loyalties or played on Messianic themes that were attractive to millennial radicals and the traditional opponents of European rule. Equipped with mimeograph machine, loudspeaker, and radio, African nationalist propaganda, whether respectable or virulent, made African villagers and townsmen politically conscious, and the parties sought to transcend traditional loyalties to tribe or kin. The experience gained by many Africans in the politics of decolonization proved valuable training for those who would subsequently take over the state machinery, and it instilled a deep feeling of commitment and idealism in the loyal party workers who saw future opportunities and careers in government and politics. The colonial administration could hardly be expected to retain the initiative before this surge of rising expectations, and with more grace than resolution the imperialists fitfully dismantled their empires.

DECOLONIZATION   The decolonization of tropical Africa began on the Gold Coast, where in 1947 Kwame Nkrumah returned as organizing secretary of the United Gold Coast Convention, founded by J. B. Danquah. The following year disturbances in the colony made a deep impression upon the British Colonial Office, which had always

regarded the Gold Coast as a model colony, and, subsequently, it accepted the recommendation of the
Watson Commission, which was investigating the Gold
Coast riots, for constitutional advance leading to self-
government. Once the commitment was made, self-
government was a matter of timing and tactics.
Kwame Nkrumah, who organized his own group in
1949, the Convention People's party, demanded immediate self-government, outbidding the more moderate Danquah for mass support, causing his own
imprisonment and martyrdom during the subsequent
civil disobedience, and ultimately winning a smashing
victory at the polls in the elections of 1951. In a
dramatic reversal of policy, in which a sense of reality
outweighed naïve insistence on principle, the British
governor of the Gold Coast, Sir Charles Arden-Clarke,
released Nkrumah from prison and invited him to
form a government. With only scattered opposition,
Nkrumah and his party emerged unchallengeable, and
with the cooperation of Arden-Clarke, who perhaps
more than any Englishman contributed to the decolonization of British Africa, Nkrumah formed an
independent African government. In 1957 Ghana, as
the Gold Coast was henceforth to be called, became
independent.

Although the Sudan had declared its independence
the year before, its ties with the Middle East and the
Arab world reduced its impact on tropical Africa
compared to that of Ghanaian independence. Despite
its small size and population, the Ghanaian self-asser-
tion became an inspiration for those Africans who had
yet to acquire self-government. As the center of Pan-
Africanism and the first to acquire political power,
Ghana had a profound impact on African intellectuals
who were encouraged to emulate Nkrumah's success.

The British now had little choice or inclination to
retard the pace of decolonization. The precedent of
Ghanaian independence destroyed virtually all reasons
to deny similar status to the other British colonies,
and the advance to independence was chiefly determined by the mechanics, not the principles, of decolonization. One by one British West African colonies be-

came independent. By 1960 rival political and regional interests had been momentarily resolved in order to achieve independence for Nigeria. Sierra Leone followed in 1961, and little Gambia in 1965.

The drive for independence in the colonies of French Africa lagged behind the independence movements in British West Africa. The pervasiveness of the lingering vestiges of the assimilation policy, the administrative centralization, and the cultural identification with France of educated Africans did not encourage talk of independence. Nevertheless, French Africans steadily gained position and influence not only in the African territories, but also in Paris, where the power of the African bloc in the Chamber of Deputies resulted in the appointment of Africans to ministerial posts. In 1956 the *Loi-Cadre*, a plan of legal and constitutional reforms for French overseas possessions, was passed by the Socialist government of Guy Mollet, granting a considerable degree of responsible government to the African territories. In the same year Morocco and Tunisia attained independence, providing example and precedent for the colonies of French West and Equatorial Africa, while the unresolved guerrilla war in Algeria convinced General Charles De Gaulle, who assumed power in 1958, not to repeat in those territories south of the Sahara the mistakes made in the decolonization of France's North African empire.

General De Gaulle envisaged a vast community of African peoples who, of their own volition, would continue the close links with France. Thus, the French Union, which had tied the colonies to France, was replaced by the French Community in which each territory was allowed to determine the nature of its membership and status in the new community. All French territories agreed to join, except Guinea. Under the firm control of Sékou Touré, Guinea demanded and received full independence in 1958. In a fit of pique the French withdrew all personnel and technical assistance, but Guinea survived, was admitted to the United Nations, and by its example made the more moderate African politicians of the other territories, who had maintained their ties with France, appear to be little more than the agents of French neocolonialism. Not surprisingly, all the various French territories achieved sovereign independence in 1960, and although some African leaders, like Léopold Senghor, sought to arrest the fragmentation of the former French empire, the proponents of territorial nationalism and sovereign status proved too strong. Togo, Cameroon, Dahomey, the Ivory Coast, Niger, Upper Volta, Mauritania, and Mali left the French Community. The Malagasy Republic, Senegal, Chad, the Central African Republic, and Gabon remained within the Community. Because it was fragmented into a host of small, relatively weak states in which the strong tradition of French culture and the overwhelming influence of France remained, former French Africa continued to exist as a cultural reality despite the independence of its many parts.

The triumph of the attainment of self-government in West and Equatorial Africa inspired African nationalists in the Congo and East Africa to press the struggle for independence. Of all the territories of tropical Africa, the Congo was perhaps the least prepared. The Belgians had ruled their colony with a benevolent despotism in which African political aspirations were diverted by economic incentives and social welfare. After World War II the Belgian government seemed resolved to keep the Congo a colony, but deep divisions between church and state within Belgium gradually sapped the determination to meet growing African demands for increasing political participation. In 1954 a liberal-Socialist coalition came to power in Belgium; it granted increasing reforms in the Congo—freedom of speech and the press and the expansion of educational opportunity—and announced a policy of "gradual emancipation." The envisioned transitional period never became a reality, however, for the Belgian authorities soon found themselves overwhelmed by criticism and events. Belgium has always contained a strong anticolonialist element, which now became more vociferous, particularly as Belgium's European allies, from whom she was traditionally aloof but was in reality dependent upon, were now in the throes of rapid decolonization. Ghana had just received independence, and General De Gaulle had announced that any French territory wanting independence should have it. Almost in a state of panic, Belgian authorities sought to catch up in the race for decolonization, and the Congo achieved independence in 1961.

Decolonization in East Africa followed a more tortuous path than in the west. European minorities lived in Kenya, Tanzania, Malawi, Rhodesia, and Zambia. These were settlers who had developed the land and, not surprisingly, were seeking to control it. In Rhodesia they were successful, receiving self-government in 1923; they remain to this day resolved not to surrender control to the African majority. Elsewhere the settlers failed to extract self-government from the imperial authorities, and although they gained privileges, they did not win control. At any given time in each territory the strongest political group invariably demanded power from the imperial authorities, while the weaker interests insisted that the imperial presence remain in the colony. Thus, during the interwar years when the white settlers were politically the most dynamic group in the colony, they demanded self-government, while the Africans urged the maintenance of imperial control. By the 1950s, however, the Africans began to seize the political initiative and demanded the end of British rule, while the settlers in East Africa looked to London for support against the African majority. They were not entirely disappointed. Not only did the imperial government crush African revolutionary uprisings, as in the case of the Mau Mau in Kenya or outbreaks of violence in Nyasaland, but it sought to devise multiracial constitutions in which interest groups were delicately balanced in multiracial governments so that no single racial group, no matter how large, would rule a colony. In this way the British sought to protect the interests of the white and Indian minorities within a democratic framework.

Not surprisingly, the Africans opposed representation based on groups, rather than individuals, and everywhere demanded "one man-one vote." Although they served as an important transitional force, the multiracial constitutions failed to provide a form of government acceptable to the Africans, and by 1960 the British government abandoned multiracial schemes, and the locus of political power immediately shifted to the Africans. In 1961 Tanganyika (Tanzania) achieved independence, followed by Kenya and Nyasaland. Uganda, which never had a large settler class, achieved independence in 1962, after internal dissension between Ganda and non-Ganda had been momentarily resolved.

In Central Africa decolonization followed a rather different course than in the east. Here, too, the British government sought to employ multiracial solutions in the form of a federation linking white Southern Rhodesia in partnership with Northern Rhodesia and Nyasaland. In the federation neither race was to dominate the other, and the obvious economic gains from such an associaton were expected to ease political tensions. Like the multiracial constitutions in East Africa, the Central African Federation could not last. The Africans in Nyasaland and Northern Rhodesia, led by Hastings Banda and Kenneth Kaunda, respectively, wanted to control their own destinies untrammeled by association with white-dominated Southern Rhodesia. Similarly, the settlers in Southern Rhodesia regarded the federation as a makeshift arrangement that restricted the expansion of their own domination of Central Africa. In 1963 the Federation was dismantled, permitting the independence of Northern Rhodesia (Zambia) and Nyasaland (Malawi) a year later. The Rhodesian government followed in 1965 by declaring itself independent from Britain, ensuring the perpetuation of settler control and white domination, but incurring the implacable hostility of independent Africa and worldwide disapproval.

By the mid-1960s, therefore, the African empires of Great Britain, France, and Belgium no longer existed. Only the Portuguese, the first European imperialists to arrive in Africa, clung tenaciously to their colonies. Of all the imperialists the Portuguese have been the most enduring, and in this sense the most successful. Like colonies elsewhere in Africa, Angola and Mozambique prospered during and after World War II. Moreover, Portuguese patriotism and pride sustained the imperial vision in Portugal; whereas, elsewhere in Europe the dream of empire gradually turned into the nightmare of decolonization. Portuguese settlers arrived in Angola and Mozambique in ever-increasing numbers, while the Portuguese security forces contained internal guerrilla resistance with a determination that neither the British nor the French could match. Whether maintaining white supremacy in Rhodesia and South Africa or sustaining Portuguese imperialism in Angola and Mozambique, decolonization in southern Africa remains distant and doubtful in this last bastion of European imperialism in Africa.

THE IMPERIAL
RECKONING

In the past men have usually marveled at the splendor of empire. This is no longer the case, but the universal denunciation of it is a rather recent phenomenon. The current moral revulsion against imperialism had its origins in the West with the acceptance of the idea that any system is immoral whose authority does not rest on the free consent of the governed. At the same time the promulgation and widespread belief in the economic interpretation of history made European imperialism in Africa appear to be a monstrous machine for exploitation in which the conquest of the continent was for the greedy purpose of acquiring riches for a few Europeans at the expense of the many Africans. In this reassessment of empire, political control was simply the means to economic ends. God and glory had no place in the search for motives. A corollary to the economic interpretation of European imperialism in Africa was the pervasive idea that the destruction of traditional African societies prevented the development of indigenous cultures and the gradual evolution of traditional institutions. This rather unsophisticated, indeed crude, interpretation of European imperialism in Africa has been widely accepted, and it inexorably presents imperialism as a monstrous evil that should be universally condemned.

The application of this or any other monolithic interpretation regrettably misses the point. The problem is more to assay the effects of the interaction between Europe and Africa, rather than to assign moral condemnation of empire on the basis of hypothesis that cannot always be supported by facts. In order to embark upon this exploration into understanding, several fundamental assumptions must be borne in mind if one is to construct an historical framework within which to place the phenomenon of European imperialism in Africa without reducing its complexities to absurd simplicities or distorting its subtleties by facile generalizations.

Despite the sudden onslaught of the scramble for Africa, the history of the partition of Africa is not without continuity with the past. The scramble was made possible by the prelude to partition earlier in the nineteenth century, just as African resistance to European imperialism was but a link in a tradition of resistance stretching from precolonial times to the African nationalist movements of the mid-twentieth century. The motivations that precipitated the partition were too complex and too conditioned by regional variations to be attributed only to excess capital and the machinations of men who manipulated it. The imperial scramble for Africa has many dimensions—strategic, political, economic, humanitarian, patriotic—which fuse together in subtle, unequal combinations at any given moment and any given place to provide the driving force for the partition.

The European partition and occupation of Africa took place at a time of enormous technological disparity between European and African societies. In many instances African technological inferiority proved decisive in the initial defeat by and subsequent resistance to European rule. Despite the impressive cultural achievements of the African past, the Africans did not experience the great scientific and technical revolution that swept through Europe in the seventeenth and eighteenth centuries, so that a great imbalance of power between European and African societies appeared by the end of the nineteenth century.

European technological supremacy was represented by not only superior weapons, but by the scientific and industrial complex to produce those weapons. Without this fundamental African weakness, European imperial conquest and control would certainly have been more hazardous and perhaps even doubtful.

Although European administration was unwanted, authoritarian, and at times despotic, the imposition of a new order on traditional African societies enabled many Africans, for better or for worse, to break away from the restrictions of these same traditional societies. In this sense, those who were ruled without consent and whose political lives were clearly limited were frequently released from the social and economic constraints of the traditional societies. In school, in church, in town, the African found new opportunities unknown in the traditional society, and although the institutions, customs, and cultures of these societies are widely admired today, to assert that if left to their own devices the Africans would have evolved new social organizations that would have been more natural, more productive, and less exploitive is little more than speculation. It is neither instructive nor useful in understanding European imperialism in Africa.

Thus, European imperialism in Africa produced many positive achievements as well as negative results. Whether the credit outweighs the debit is in the attitudes and assumptions of the beholder and is consequently impossible to determine in any absolute sense. Rather than view imperialism in Africa as a balance sheet of good and evil, the establishment and administration of European empire should be regarded as a process that for all its real or imaginary evils involved an unparalleled diffusion of culture. This is perhaps the historic meaning of European imperialism and the very essence of empire in Africa. Europeans brought new economic, social, administrative, and scientific techniques. Equally important, they brought new ideas that were adopted, molded, and shaped in part by Europeans, but principally by Africans to fit African conditions and to fulfill African needs. In a historic sense, this enorm   cultural diffusion ended the old Africa and began the new. History will do better to abstain from pronouncing a moral judgment on European imperialism in Africa and might attempt instead to understand the means and ends of this process called "imperialism," which forms that European interlude between the African past and the African future.

Bibliography

Chapter 1: The Portuguese in Africa

* Chilcote, Ronald H. *Portuguese in Africa*. Englewood Cliffs, N.J.: Prentice-Hall, 1967.

* Duffy, James. *Portugal in Africa*. Cambridge, Mass.: Harvard University Press, 1962.

Hammond, Richard J. *Portugal in Africa, 1515–1910*. Stanford, Calif.: Stanford University Press, 1966.

Chapter 2: Africa Before the Scramble

Ajayi, J. F. Ade. *Christian Missions in Nigeria, 1831–1881*. Evanston, Ill.: Northwestern University Press, 1965.

Ayandale, E. A. *The Missionary Impact on Modern Nigeria*. Evanston, Ill.: Northwestern University Press, 1967.

Curtin, Philip. *The Atlantic Slave Trade: A Census*. Madison, Wis.: University of Wisconsin Press, 1969.

* Davidson, Basil. *The African Slave Trade*. Boston: Little, Brown, 1961.

Groves, C. P. *The Planting of Christianity in Africa*. London: Lutterworth Press, 1964.

Hallett, Robin. *The Penetration of Africa*. New York: Praeger, 1965.

* Moorehead, Alan. *The White Nile*. New York: Praeger, 1965.

* ———. *The Blue Nile*. London: Hamish Hamilton, 1962.

Oliver, Roland. *The Missionary Factor in East Africa*. London: Longmans, Green, 1952.

Rotberg, Robert I. *Christian Missionaries and the Creation of Northern Rhodesia 1880–1924*. Princeton: Princeton University Press, 1965.

Chapter 3: Partition and Pacification

Anstey, Roger. *Britain and the Congo in the Nineteenth Century*. Oxford: Clarendon Press, 1962.

Collins, Robert O. *King Leopold, England, and the Upper Nile, 1898–1909*. New Haven: Yale University Press, 1968.

---

* Available in paperback.

* ———— (ed.). *The Partition of Africa: Illusion or Necessity*. New York: Wiley, 1969.

Cookey, S. J. S. *Britain and the Congo Question, 1885–1913*. New York: Humanities Press, 1968.

Crowe, S. E. *The Berlin West Africa Conference*. London: Longmans, Green, 1942.

Flint, J. E. *Sir George Goldie*. London: Oxford University Press, 1960.

Hargreaves, J. D. *Prelude to the Partition of Africa*. London: Macmillan, 1963.

Kanya-Forstner, A. S. *The Conquest of the Western Sudan*. Cambridge: Cambridge University Press, 1969.

Langer, William L. *The Diplomacy of Imperialism, 1890–1902*. New York: Knopf, 1935.

Lockhart, J. G. and C. M. Woodhouse. *Rhodes*. London: Macmillan, 1963.

Oliver, Roland. *Sir Harry Johnston and the Scramble for Africa*. London: St. Martins Press, 1957.

Perham, Dame Margery. *Lugard*. London: Collins, 1960.

* Robinson, Ronald and John Gallagher. *Africa and the Victorians: The Official Mind of Imperialism*. London: Macmillan, 1961.

Sanderson, G. N. *England, Europe, and the Upper Nile, 1882–1899*. Edinburgh: Edinburgh University Press, 1965.

Taylor, A. J. P. *Germany's First Bid for Colonies, 1884–1885*. London: Macmillan, 1938.

Chapter 4: European Rule

A. Britain in Africa

Bourret, F. M. *The Gold Coast*. Stanford, Calif.: Stanford University Press, 1949.

Cook, A. N. *British Enterprise in Nigeria*. Philadelphia: University of Pennsylvania Press, 1943.

Fyfe, C. *History of Sierra Leone*. London: Oxford University Press, 1962.

Gailey, Harry A. *A History of Gambia*. New York: Praeger, 1965.

Gann, L. H. *A History of Northern Rhodesia*. New York: Humanities Press, 1964.

————. *A History of Southern Rhodesia*. New York: Humanities Press, 1965.

Hailey, Lord. *An African Survey*. London: Oxford University Press, 1957.

Heussler, Robert. *Yesterday's Rulers*. Syracuse: Syracuse University Press, 1963.

Low, D. A., and R. C. Pratt. *Buganda and British Overrule*. London: Oxford University Press, 1960.

Perham, Margery. *Native Administration in Nigeria*. London: Oxford University Press, 1937.

Taylor, J. Clagett. *The Political Development of Tanganyika*. Stanford, Calif.: Stanford University Press, 1966.

B. France in Africa

Betts, Raymond F. *Assimilation and Association in French Colonial Policy, 1890–1914*. New York: Columbia University Press, 1961.

* Brace, Richard M. *Morocco, Algeria, Tunisia*. Englewood Cliffs, N.J.: Prentice-Hall, 1964.

Brunschwig, Henri. *French Colonialism, 1871–1914: Myths and Realities*. New York: Praeger, 1966.

Crowder, Michael. *Senegal, A Study in French Assimilation Policy*. London: Methuen, 1967.

* Hargreaves, J. D. *West Africa: The Former French States*. Englewood Cliffs, N.J.: Prentice-Hall, 1967.

Roberts, S. H. *History of French Colonial Policy, 1870–1925*. 2 vols. London: P. S. King and Son, 1929.

C. Germany in Africa

Henderson, W. O. *Studies in German Colonial History*. Chicago: Quadrangle Books, 1962.

Iliffe, John. *Tanganyika Under German Rule, 1905–1912*. Cambridge: Cambridge University Press, 1969.

Louis, William R. *Ruanda-Urundi, 1884–1919*. Oxford: Clarendon Press, 1963.

———. *Great Britain and Germany's Lost Colonies, 1914–1919*. Oxford: Clarendon Press, 1967.

———. *Britain and Germany in Africa*. New Haven: Yale University Press, 1967.

Rudin, Harry R. *Germany in the Cameroons, 1884–1914*. New Haven: Yale University Press, 1938.

D. Belgium in Africa

Anstey, Roger. *King Leopold's Legacy*. London: Oxford University Press, 1966.

* Brausch, Georges. *Belgian Administration in the Congo*. London: Oxford University Press, 1961.

Slade, Ruth. *King Leopold's Congo*. London: Oxford University Press, 1962.

E. South Africa

The Cambridge History of the British Empire, Vol. VIII, *South Africa, Rhodesia, and the High Commission Territories*. Cambridge: Cambridge University Press, 1963.

* De Kiewiet, C. W. *A History of South Africa, Social and Economic*. Oxford: Clarendon Press, 1941.

Macmillan, W. M. *Bantu, Boer, and Briton*. Oxford: Clarendon Press, 1963.

Wilson, Monica and Leonard Thompson. *The Oxford History of South Africa*. London: Oxford University Press, 1969.

Chapter 5:   Dismantling the Empires

Apter, D. E. *The Gold Coast in Transition*. Princeton: Princeton University Press, 1955.

Coleman, J. S. *Nigeria: A Background to Nationalism*. Berkeley, Calif.: University of California Press, 1958.

* Hodgkin, Thomas L. *Nationalism in Colonial Africa*. New York: New York University Press, 1957.

—— and Ruth Schachter. *French-Speaking West Africa in Transition*. New York: Columbia University Press, 1961.

* Sithole, Ndabaningi. *African Nationalism*. London: Oxford University Press, 1968.

Chronology

1415–1460	Prince Henry the Navigator directs Portuguese exploration of West African coast
1488	Bartholomeu Dias rounds the Cape of Good Hope
1498	Vasco de Gama voyages to India and visits Swahili city-states in East Africa
16th century	Portuguese ascendency on the coasts of Africa
1510	Organized slave trade begins between Africa and the Americas
1600–1650	Dutch ascendency on the African coast and in the Orient
1652	Dutch found Cape Town
1650–1713	Rivalry among Dutch, French, and English for dominance in the African trade
1713–1815	Anglo-French rivalry in Africa and the world
1772	Slavery is abolished in England
1787	Freetown settled by freed slaves
1788	British establish the African Association to promote exploration
1791	Sierra Leone Company founded
1797–1832	Park, Clapperton, Denham, and the Lander brothers explore the Niger River and exterior of West Africa
1798	Napoleon conquers Egypt
1807	British Parliament declares slave trade illegal and begins struggle to end the trade
1836	The Great Trek extends Boer settlement in South Africa
1854	Effectiveness of quinine against malaria enables Europeans to enter African interior
1854–1865	French begin expansion from Senegal into the West Sudan
1856–1875	Burton, Speke, Livingstone, and Stanley seek the source of the Nile River
1861	British annex Lagos
1876	King Leopold II establishes African International Association
1882	British invade Egypt
1884–1885	Berlin Conference establishes guidelines for partition
1885–1914	Partition, conquest, and pacification

Index

The text of this book was set on the Linotype in Garamond (No. 3), a modern rendering of the type first cut by Claude Garamond (1510–1561). Garamond was a pupil of Geoffroy Troy and is believed to have based his letters on the Venetian models, although he introduced a number of important differences, and it is to him we owe the letter which we know as old-style. He gave to his letters a certain elegance and a feeling of movement that won for their creator an immediate reputation and the patronage of Francis I of France.

Composed, printed, and bound by The Colonial Press Inc., Clinton, Massachusetts. Typography and cover design by Elton Robinson. Cover map by Robert Cordes.